Redeemed

That You May Know God
and Who You Are in Jesus Christ

Ladonna Will

CLAY BRIDGES
PRESS

Redeemed

That You May Know God and Who You Are in Jesus Christ

Copyright © 2020 by Ladonna Will

Published by Clay Bridges in Houston, TX
www.ClayBridgesPress.com

Unless otherwise indicated, all Scripture quotations are taken from the New American Standard Bible® (NASB), Copyright © 1960, 1962, 1963, 1968, 1971, 1972, 1973, 1975, 1977, 1995 by The Lockman Foundation. Used by permission. www.Lockman.org.

Scripture quotations marked (KJV) are taken from the King James Version (KJV): King James Version, public domain.

Scripture quotations marked (HCSB) are taken from the Holman Christian Standard Bible®, Copyright © 1999, 2000, 2002, 2003, 2009 by Holman Bible Publishers. Used by permission. HCSB® is a federally registered trademark of Holman Bible Publishers.

ISBN: 978-1-953300-10-2
eISBN: 978-1-953300-05-8

Special Sales: Clay Bridges titles are available in wholesale quantity. Please visit www.claybridgesbulk.com to order 10 or more copies at a retail discount. Custom imprinting or excerpting can also be done to fit special needs. Contact Clay Bridges at Info@ClayBridgesPress.com.

This book is dedicated to
God the Father, Son, and Holy Spirit.
May the message further the Kingdom of God
and be a blessing to all who read it.
Thank You, Lord, for loving us so much that
You gave Your all to make us Your own!

Special Thanks

I give special thanks to Harold, my husband. You spent numerous hours patiently listening as I read you the chapters of *Redeemed*. You encouraged me from the start and helped me to the finish line. Thank you for being a wonderful companion throughout the story of my life.

To our son, Todd—it is always such a joy to talk with you about our mutual walk with God. Thank you for believing in my vision and for loving the Lord with all your heart.

Thank you, Melissha Hill. You read my manuscript from beginning to end and gave me valuable input on how it reads. I appreciate your candid opinions and suggestions that helped produce a better end result.

Tony Krishack, thank you for your encouragement and interest in this book. Your involvement was a big help along the way.

Finally, to the Lucid Books team, thank you for believing in me and seeing the potential in the message *Redeemed* tells. May you have many jewels in your heavenly crown!

Table of Contents

God's Song to Us

I call you into My house
And set you before My throne.
I tell you that I love you
And make you My very own.

Introduction

Early in 2018, I started reading and meditating on the book of Romans. I was saved in 1971 by means of this wonderful portion of the scriptures. However, after all those years, as I read Romans over and over, the Lord began to show me new things I had not seen before, and I realized that God wanted me to put what He was revealing in book form.

The scope of *Redeemed* is the redemption plan of God through Jesus Christ from before the foundation of the world, throughout history, and into eternity. It examines the different phases of that plan and the importance of God maintaining His righteous character as He deals with His creation through two different approaches: first as a just judge through the administration of His law and then as a gracious, loving Father through the redeeming blood of His Son, Jesus Christ.

It was always God's desire to have the intimacy of a father-son relationship. After the failure of many of the sons of His first creation, God designed a new plan to ensure success for His subsequent creation. The new plan would be very costly, but in His great love, He gave everything He had to make it a reality. My prayer is that the words of this book will bring a greater insight into the treasure God offers so that you will know Him and know who you are in Christ.

Chapter 1
My Own Story

I am an ordinary person, recreated in Jesus and made into a son of God. I grew up in Ohio in a family of four—my parents and sister and me. We had a good life with good times together. I excelled in school and graduated from high school and went to work in a legal office as a secretary. A few days after graduation, I met my husband-to-be, Harold. A year later, we were married. I was nineteen, and he was twenty-three. June 2020 marks our fiftieth wedding anniversary.

We were attending the church where I would come to know the Lord. I had questions about life and was looking for answers. Someone told me that if I didn't know for sure that I was going to heaven, I was not. I pondered the idea a lot and wondered how anyone could possibly know that. I was lost and didn't even know it. I was reading my Bible without much understanding, but I came across one scripture that I took to heart: "Ask, and it will be given to you; seek, and you will find; knock, and it will be opened to you" (Matthew 7:7). I started asking for answers.

Early one September day when I was twenty, I was at home by myself without any way to contact the rest of my family—this was before cell phones. Suddenly, I had a vision of myself falling into a deep, dark tunnel. As I descended, the walls were dark and lifeless all around me. Yet, I sensed an eerie presence—not human or animal, but otherworldly, demonic. I knew that I was falling into hell. I felt so alone and knew I was eternally separated from God. It shook me and scared me to my very core. I came out of the vision and frantically grabbed my Bible. The book of Romans opened, and I began to read the first six chapters. It made no sense to me, but I was able to calm down a bit.

For a week I walked around in a stunned state, not knowing what to think or do. But after that week, I went to the home of my choir director for a Bible study. His brother LaVon, a Pentecostal pastor, was in town to lead the study. LaVon opened his Bible and started to teach the first six chapters of Romans. He told the salvation message of Jesus Christ and how He had paid my way. I did not have to do it myself by being good enough. I believed it and was saved right then and there. No one else knew, but I had become a new creation in Jesus Christ. The Holy Spirit became my Helper and Friend. Believe me; I needed Him. I wouldn't have made it this far without Him.

Over the next few years, God gave Harold and me two sons, Kevin and Todd. We moved to Texas for new opportunities when Kevin was two and Todd was five weeks old. We never dreamed we could own a house, but within six months, we bought our first home in Houston. Harold worked as an automotive technician, and I was a stay-at-home mom. We did our best at being parents, but it certainly was a journey. We were active in our church and were learning more about the Lord.

I took classes in Evangelism Explosion and learned how to share the salvation message. I am forever grateful to the Holy Spirit for the many opportunities He has given me to lead family, friends, coworkers, and strangers to receive Jesus as their Savior. He worked on their hearts and opened them to believe.

When the boys were going into the second and fourth grades, I was very concerned about their level of learning in a public school. I believed the Lord was leading me to homeschool our boys. We worked through learning disabilities and getting caught up to acceptable levels of achievement based on standardized testing. We all learned together, especially me as I discovered things about myself and what the Holy Spirit could be to me.

One thing I uncovered about myself was that I lacked a great deal of patience. I became easily frustrated with the boys and easily angered. Things were just not going the way I wanted. No matter how hard I tried to change my behavior by my own determination, I had no success. I finally told the Lord that I had no patience and just couldn't do what I needed to do. I asked His forgiveness for the umpteenth time and asked Him if He would be my patience, and I left it in His hands. I rested and He supernaturally became my patience. Praise God for His ability to change people and things!

I still had some control issues because I wanted MY family to be the ideal Christian family. I was disappointed that Harold and the boys weren't very interested in church and things of the Lord. They were mostly going along with me to humor me. Kevin became rebellious as he reached his late teens, and Todd was just kind of there. It was not a happy time. I knew there had to be more in my Christian walk, and I thought a close family friend was acting strangely ever since he was baptized in the Holy Spirit. I started asking God for His help again to show me about being baptized in the Holy Spirit. By that time, I had been saved for twenty-seven years, but the churches we had been a part of did not believe in the Holy Spirit's baptism, at least not for our present day.

With our friends, Harold and I went to a forty-day, citywide prayer event called Prayer Mountain, which was held in Houston. There, I encountered the touch of the Holy Spirit for the first time and experienced His power. I was hungry for more. My life was in need of His mending. At one of the meetings, the Lord showed me that my disappointment with my family was, in reality, a disappointment with Him. That grieved my heart, and I repented. In His grace, God showed me what I did not realize about myself, and it changed my life.

When Prayer Mountain was over, I sought out the meeting place where the organizers of the prayer event regularly got together. They met frequently in a Marriott hotel in the Galleria on weekend evenings under the ministry of Doug Stringer. On January 3, 1997, I went to the meeting with our close friends, determined to be baptized in the Holy Spirit. The rest of my family was not interested in going. The Pensacola, Florida, revival was happening at that time, and a lady from the Brownsville church was at the January 3 meeting, ministering with Doug Stringer in Houston. She prayed for me and laid hands on me, and I was gloriously baptized in the Holy Spirit, receiving God's gift of speaking in tongues.

Talk about a transformation! I was so happy and had a new perspective. Harold, Kevin, and Todd were amazed at the change. Todd was the first to be drawn to the events being done by the Spirit. He and I decided to go to Pensacola, along with another family, to experience what God was doing there. It was marvelous! While we were there, Todd was born again and baptized in the Spirit. When we came home, our house was full of joy, and before long Harold joined in our adventure. After twenty-seven years of marriage, he encountered God, was saved, and baptized in the Holy Spirit.

Kevin was away at college, living a rebellious lifestyle. He came home and was astonished at the change of atmosphere in our home. It was not like that at the home where he was staying. While we talked about what we had experienced, a demon manifested and tried to kill Kevin. At first, we didn't know what to do, but God in His grace showed us the steps to take to stop the attack. The next day, we took Kevin for ministry to one of God's servants. Kevin too was born again and baptized in the Holy Spirit. Talk about a change in him! Salvation and baptism in the Holy Spirit were truly miracles for our whole family. Our relationships were healed and turned around. The most memorable time I cherish is the time we all went to Pensacola and enjoyed the presence of the Lord together—time in worship and communion and time together as a family enjoying the beautiful beach and eating together after the services.

It is not my habit to journal, but during this special time in Pensacola, I documented some of the wonderful things God was doing. Of special importance later on, I noted that on May 29, 1997, God showed Kevin how very much He loves him. Over the years, we often met together to pray in the Spirit and to commune with God and each other.

Harold was a heavy smoker. He enjoyed smoking. He had smoked since his preteens—for over forty years. I had always wanted him to quit, but that had to be his decision. It was 1999. One day, I started to agree with God's Word in Mark 11:22–24 where it says:

> *And Jesus answered saying to them, "Have faith in God. Truly I say to you, whoever says to this mountain, 'Be taken up and cast into the sea,' and does not doubt in his heart, but believes that what he says is going to happen, it will be* granted *him. Therefore I say to you, all things for which you pray and ask, believe that you have received them, and they will be* granted *you."*

When I was alone, I started saying that Harold was a nonsmoker and that he did not like the taste of cigarettes. Harold had a doctor's appointment a couple of days later, and the doctor told him he needed to quit smoking. He prescribed a patch for Harold. I didn't say a word to Harold about not smoking, but thought, *Hmmmm*. Well, the patch didn't do anything but make Harold smoke more. I just kept agreeing with the Lord. After about a week, Harold told the Lord (not me, mind you) that he wasn't able to quit smoking and that he needed His help. God told Harold that if he took the first step, He would finish it. Harold took the pack of cigarettes and threw them away. God met him there at the place of faith. Suddenly, Harold had no desire for cigarettes and had no withdrawal symptoms. A few days later, he told me he hadn't smoked a cigarette for a number of days. In a matter of ten days, he had stopped smoking and has not touched a cigarette since. God awesomely honored Harold's faith and mine. Thank You, Holy Spirit, for Your miraculous help!

The Holy Spirit has faithfully been our helper since we were saved. Sometimes His help has been truly miraculous. Whether through miraculous or natural paths, the Spirit always leads us in the way we should go. The Spirit's help is supernatural, done in His power and not our own. He has helped us through good times and bad, to bring us victory over the flesh, the world, and the devil.

A year after Harold quit smoking, he experienced congestive heart failure, became disabled, and had to quit work. That was a change for me, as I had to go back to work full-time to support us. God had prepared a way for us, as I had been working part-time for a few years to help put Todd through private high school. During that time, I learned a new trade in real estate. I was able to use what I had learned to bring in the needed income.

God is our provider, and He has given us what we need. One of the first things I asked God to do after I was saved was from a verse I found in James: "But if any of you lacks wisdom, let him ask of God, who gives to all generously and without reproach, and it will be given to him" (James 1:5). God has honored that request through the years and given us wisdom on how to live and act in various situations. That is especially true in finances and health, enabling us to prosper under His direction.

As time passed, the devil made his share of attacks against our family, but the Holy Spirit has faithfully helped us, and God has opened the way to make all things work together for our good.

Harold's health continued to decline from 2000 to 2014. He had many operations and hospital stays. When the outlook for his heart was rapidly declining, God opened the way for a heart transplant. It has been over five years since he received a new heart. Thank you, Lord, for the gift that young man and You gave us.

Kevin was not satisfied with his career in the banking world, so he made a change into law enforcement. He found his niche and was on the Houston police force for two years when we received a knock on our door. In 2011, Kevin was doing an accident investigation on the highway when he was struck and killed by a drunk driver. He went quickly to be with his Lord and Savior. We are so thankful that he had become a son of God and that we will be with him again when all the sons of God are revealed. I later looked back on my journaling from fourteen years earlier and realized that Kevin went home to the arms of Jesus on May 29, 2011, on the anniversary of when God first whispered His love for Kevin into his heart. Now Kevin is experiencing that love face-to-face.

Once again, our Helper, the Holy Spirit, got us through this time of sorrow. By the grace of God, He kept bitterness against the drunk driver from getting down in our hearts. We did not have to deal with the heavy burden that bitterness would have put on our hearts and lives. Even though we missed Kevin terribly, we decided to go on in love and determination to be happy again. By the Holy Spirit, I was able to tell the defendant and the entire court at the criminal trial for Kevin's death the message of salvation through the blood of Jesus Christ. What the enemy meant for evil, God turned around and gave many opportunities to share Jesus with others.

Shortly after Kevin's death, Todd became ill, and we learned that he had *leukemia*. God opened a way to treat his illness, and he is doing well.

God just recently derailed the plans of the enemy again for me. After having surgery, it was discovered that I had the earliest signs of cancer, but it has been completely removed. If I had not gone in for corrective surgery, I would not have known, and it would not have been dealt with.

This is my story. It is not over yet. My Father loves me so much. He proved it when He sent Jesus, and He proved it again when He sent the Holy Spirit. He loves you too so that you can write your own story through Him.

Chapter 2

God's Nature

If I could describe the character of God in one word, I would say that He is *righteous*. That one word encompasses so much that if we get a clearer grasp on what it entails, it can open up a broader understanding of the scriptures. God's righteousness defines every aspect of His character and what He does: His justice, sternness, judgment, and wrath; His holiness, forbearance, mercy, forgiveness, faithfulness, goodness, and love. It explains the way He interacts with us. Understanding God's righteousness is key to understanding the Bible and to understanding how God operates.

So how should we define *righteous*? Simply put, it means being fully right, above blame, unable to be found wrong. A righteous being is above judgment, without any guilt or condemnation for any actions whatsoever. He is just, fair, pure, true, and faultless. No one can prove him to be otherwise. A righteous person is counted legally right. No law can condemn him.

The scriptures speak extensively about the righteousness of God. God is undeniably righteous and has never done anything wrong. Look at these statements:

> *For You have upheld my just cause; You are seated on Your throne as a righteous judge. . . . But the LORD sits enthroned forever; He has established His throne for judgment. He judges the world with righteousness; He executes judgment on the nations with fairness.*
>
> —Ps. 9:4, 7– 8 HCSB

> *For the LORD is righteous; He loves righteous deeds. The upright will see His face.*
>
> —Ps. 11:7 HCSB

God holds Himself legally to a standard of perfect righteousness. He always says what He means. We can believe whatever He says because He consistently speaks the unchanging truth. He is Truth. He absolutely will not lie. He is true to His word and lives up to it always.

> *Let God be found true, though every man* be found *a liar, as it is written, "THAT YOU MAY BE JUSTIFIED IN YOUR WORDS, AND PREVAIL WHEN YOU ARE JUDGED." . . . The God who inflicts wrath is not unrighteous, is He? . . . May it never be! For otherwise how will God judge the world?*
>
> —Rom. 3:4–6

The Bible makes it clear that God is righteous. Not only is He righteous, but He expects His creation to be righteous. He is the standard that everything and everyone is measured against, and He wants to have a relationship with creatures who have a nature like His.

The Bible brings forth the standard for such a relationship: "Lord, who can dwell in Your tent? Who can live on Your holy mountain? The one who lives honestly, practices righteousness, and acknowledges the truth in his heart" (Psalm 15:1–2 HCSB). Wow! Who can live up to that standard? Yes, God does not lie and cannot. But people are another story. We know how to put on a good act. We do lie. We want to be found right, but we lie to hide the fact that we are not, so we can make ourselves look right. In many ways, we fail to be righteous.

To be righteous like God is a challenging expectation. God wants us to have revelation of how to walk in fulfillment of this expectation. This book is dedicated to the Father's purpose so that we may know Him and walk in the great love and destiny He has for us.

The Bible states the wonderful hope and plan that God has prepared for us:

> *Behold, what manner of love the Father hath bestowed upon us, that we should be called the sons of God. . . . Beloved, now are we the sons of God, and it doth not yet appear what we shall be: but we know that, when he [Jesus] shall appear,* **we shall be like him**; *for we shall see him as he is."* (emphasis added)
>
> —1 John 3:1–2 KJV

Let's begin that adventure!

Chapter 3

The Original Creation

W e have limited knowledge of the original creation. One thing is evident. God wanted fellowship with beings that were like Him and could love Him freely of their own choice.

A fact that is important to our understanding God's nature is that God is a spiritual being. John 4:24 says that "God is spirit, and those who worship Him must worship in spirit and truth." The first beings God created to have fellowship with Him were spiritual beings like Him. Psalm 148:1–6 (HCSB) tell of God's creation of the heavenly realm:

> *Hallelujah! Praise the LORD from the heavens; praise Him in the heights. Praise Him, all His angels; praise Him, all His hosts. Praise Him, sun and moon; praise Him, all you shining stars. Praise Him, highest heavens, and you waters above the heavens. Let them praise the name of Yahweh, for* **He commanded, and they were created**. *He set them in position forever and ever; He gave an order that will never pass away.* (emphasis added)

Heavenly beings do not have natural bodies like we have. Although we may find it hard to understand, they have spiritual bodies with spiritual capabilities. The Bible tells us that in heaven there are angels and living creatures and the host of heaven. The term *host* refers to a large number and talks about the army of God consisting of innumerable angels. *Host* can also refer to the large number of created heavenly bodies including the sun, moon, and stars. However, we will not discuss that aspect of the host of heaven since it is another whole study in itself.

So, let's examine what the Bible tells us about these spiritual beings.

Angels

First, we will talk about angels. Angels were beautiful and perfect when God made them. No flaw or unrighteousness was in them; they were fitting companions for God. Let's look at some of their characteristics:

- Angels were created by God—Psalm 148 quoted above.
- They are spirit beings and have a service ministry/function. "And of the angels he saith, Who maketh his angels spirits, and his ministers a flame of fire" (Hebrews 1:7 KJV).
- Angels have a free will and can choose to love and obey God or reject Him.
- Angels can fly. "Then I saw another angel flying high overhead" (Revelation 14:6 HCSB).
- They are wise. "And my lord is wise, according to the wisdom of an angel of God" (2 Samuel 14:20 KJV).
- They are powerful and execute God's commandments. "Bless the LORD, you His angels, mighty in strength, who perform His word, obeying the voice of His word" (Psalm 103:20)!
- They are humble. "Yet Michael the archangel, when he was disputing with the Devil in a debate about Moses' body, did not dare bring an abusive condemnation against him but said, 'The Lord rebuke you'" (Jude 9 HCSB)!

- Angels are spiritual beings and cannot die. They are sexless and do not reproduce. They are eternal. They live permanently in the spiritual condition they choose. If they sin, they become eternally corrupted. There is no way to redeem them. If they choose obedience and righteousness, they remain in that holy condition.

> *The sons of this age [people] marry and are given in marriage, but those who are considered worthy to attain to that age and the resurrection from the dead [people who will be counted worthy to receive eternal life],* **neither marry nor are given in marriage; for they cannot even die anymore, because they are like angels,** *and are sons of God.* (emphasis added)
>
> —Luke 20:34–36

- Angels are holy. "When the Son of man shall come in his glory, and all the **holy angels** with him, then shall he sit upon the throne of his glory" (Matthew 25:31 KJV). (emphasis added)
- Angels are innumerable. "But ye are come unto mount Sion [Zion], and unto the city of the living God, the heavenly Jerusalem, and to an **innumerable company of angels**" (Hebrews 12:22 KJV). (emphasis added)
- Angels can take on human form. "Do not neglect to show hospitality to strangers, for by this some have entertained angels without knowing it" (Hebrews 13:2).
- Even though angels can take on the appearance of human form for earthly assignments, they are spirit and have no flesh or blood.
- They have access between heaven and earth. "He [Jacob] had a dream, and behold, a ladder was set on the earth with its top reaching to heaven; and behold, the angels of God were ascending and descending on it" (Genesis 28:12).

- They have emotions. "In the same way, I tell you, there is joy in the presence of the angels of God over one sinner who repents" (Luke 15:10).

Angels, being one of God's first creations, existed before there were any people. The Bible tells of the angels being present and rejoicing at the creation of the earth. Angels witnessed the creation of plants, animals, and people. In Job, the earliest biblical account to be written, God questions Job about his knowledge of the creation:

> *Where were you when I established the earth? Tell Me, if you have understanding. Who fixed its dimensions? . . . Or who laid its cornerstone while the morning stars sang together and all the sons of God shouted for joy?*
>
> —Job 38:4–7 HCSB

Here, we see that "morning stars" is another name for "sons of God." Sons of God is a name applied only to beings that have the same nature or "genes" of their Father, God. This is important to remember as we continue to look at more of the beings God created. In this case, Father God is Spirit, so the sons must also be of the same Spirit. It takes a direct divine, specific act of God to create a son of God. The angels are spirit beings created directly by God and are considered sons of God. These sons were able to watch the creation of our habitat take place and rejoice about it.

There are different classes of angels according to their offices and functions. Some serve as messengers, others as warriors. They are ministers, worshipers, and executors of God's Word. They stand by God's throne and bow before Him. We will look briefly at their ranks as mentioned in scripture:

- Seraphim – The word *seraphim* comes from the verb *saraph*, meaning "to burn" in the context of burning up what is not holy. Seraphim constantly pronounce the holiness of God before His throne, and no sin can come into God's presence. Obviously, seraphim are pure and righteous before God and guard against any unrighteousness coming into God's presence. The only account of seraphim is in this passage from Isaiah, which shows them worshiping God; they attend God's throne and are constantly in His presence:

I saw the Lord sitting on a throne, lofty and exalted, with the train of His robe filling the temple. Seraphim stood above Him, each having six wings: with two he covered his face, and with two he covered his feet, and with two he flew. And one called out to another and said, "Holy, Holy, Holy, is the LORD of hosts, the whole earth is full of His glory." And the foundations of the thresholds trembled at the voice of him who called out, while the temple was filling with smoke. Then I said, "Woe is me, for I am ruined! Because I am a man of unclean lips, and I live among a people of unclean lips; for my eyes have seen the King, the LORD of hosts." Then one of the seraphim flew to me, with a burning coal in his hand, which he had taken from the altar with tongs. He touched my mouth with it and said, "Behold, this has touched your lips; and your iniquity is taken away and your sin is forgiven."

—Isa. 6:1–7

In this passage of scripture, the prophet Isaiah has a vision of the throne of God. Upon seeing it, Isaiah recognizes that his own unrighteousness disqualifies him from coming into God's presence. The seraphim immediately act to cleanse the sin from Isaiah so that the prophet can encounter God and receive the assignment that God has for him.

- Archangel – An archangel is widely considered to be a chief angel. In the Bible, only Michael is specifically named as an archangel (Jude 1:9). First Thessalonians 4:16 talks about Jesus returning to earth with the voice of the archangel but does not designate a specific name of the archangel. Daniel 10:13 describes Michael as "one of the chief princes," so there could be more than one archangel; some think this classification possibly includes Gabriel. Daniel 12:1 describes Michael as "the great prince who stands *guard*." Michael's role appears to be that of a protective, warring angel. Whereas, Gabriel functions frequently as a messenger, but also as one who assists Michael.

- Cherubim (cherub, singular) – Cherubim are powerful guardian angels—a far cry from the fat little babies depicted by our society. They praise, bless, and adore the Lord. In Eden, they guarded the way to the tree of life (Genesis 3:24). Ezekiel 10 describes them as having four wings, four faces, and whirling wheels. They are covered with eyes, look out for God's interests, and are the guardians of God's throne. They are the royal guard.

  When the nation of Israel was instructed to make the Ark of the Covenant, God had them make two images of cherubim to place over the mercy seat of the Ark of the Covenant (Exodus 25: 18–20) to represent God's protection of His covenant with man. Psalm 34:7 says, "The angel of the LORD encamps around those who fear Him, and rescues them."

- Messengers – Messengers are described in Luke 2:8–14. The Hebrew word for a messenger is *mal'ak*.[1] It is also the word for angel. Being messengers is one of the chief functions of angels.

---

1. James L. Strong, *The New Strong's Exhaustive Concordance of the Bible* (Nashville, TN: Thomas Nelson Publishers, 1990), "Strong's 4397, Malak."

The role of angels initially appears to have been focused on things pertaining to worship, adoration, and fellowship with God and on carrying out heavenly administration. Later, when human beings came on the scene, that role expanded to include ministry to mankind. There are numerous biblical accounts of their help. In Genesis 21, an angel helped Hagar when she fled into the wilderness and was dying from thirst. Angels often delivered messages of instruction, revelation, and hope to people. We specifically point out the angels who told the shepherds of Jesus's birth and Gabriel who came to Mary to tell her she would bear the Savior of the world.

Living Creatures

Living creatures are another spiritual creation of God. They are awesome creatures appearing only around the throne of God. The full description of their appearance can be found in Ezekiel 1. Here I will quote just a part of the long passage:

> *The form of four living creatures came from it [from a cloud flashing with fire]. And this was their appearance: They had human form, but each of them had four faces and four wings. Their legs were straight, and the soles of their feet were like the hooves of a calf, sparkling like the gleam of polished bronze. They had human hands under their wings on their four sides. All four of them had faces and wings. Their wings were touching. The creatures did not turn as they moved; each one went straight ahead. The form of each of their faces was that of a man, and each of the four had the face of a lion on the right, the face of an ox on the left, and the face of an eagle. That is what their faces were like. Their wings were spread upward; each had two wings touching that of another and two wings covering its body. Each creature went straight ahead. Wherever the Spirit wanted to go, they went without turning as they moved. The form*

of the living creatures was like the appearance of burning coals of fire and torches. Fire was moving back and forth between the living creatures; it was bright, with lightning coming out of it.

—Ezekiel 1:5–13 HCSB

The living creatures give glory, honor, and thanks to the One seated on the throne, leading the worship in heaven. In the book of Revelation, we see them involved in directing judgment against the enemies of God.

Chapter 4

An Angel Gone Bad (The Fall of Spiritual Beings)

We have already said that spiritual beings were created perfect, without flaw. No evil was known or existed in heaven in the presence of God. There was no corruption, sickness, pain, or death. Unhappiness, sadness, and fear were unknown. Selfishness did not exist. There was no darkness. Only sweet fellowship and joy were experienced by all. Love was enjoyed, freely given, and received. Yes, spiritual beings are eternal, and this was the wonderful state God created for them to live in forever. But something happened.

The Word of God says that "God is love" (1 John 4:8). Even though God pours out amazing love on His entire creation, He does not force His sons to love Him. Just as we want other people to love us by choice, so does God desire His sons to love Him by their own volition. From the beginning, spiritual beings had the choice to receive God's love or to reject Him—to love Him or not to love Him. Love doesn't mean much if it is not given freely.

Love expresses itself through obedience in its desire to please another. Those who love God will keep His commands, and His commands are a joy, not a burden. God gives His commands out of love to protect His sons for their good. Consider the simple analogy of a parent who tells his child to not play in the street so the child will not be harmed by oncoming traffic. The parent is not being mean but knows more than the child and wants to protect him. By disobeying, the child opens himself up to trouble, even if he doesn't understand why he has been told to stay out of the street.

Let's look at one of the head angels as he was when God created him. God formed a very wonderful angel and named him Lucifer. It is highly possible that Lucifer was an archangel. In Ezekiel 28, we are told many of Lucifer's qualities. He was perfect, full of wisdom, and he was beautiful. He must have been absolutely stunning as he was covered with precious stones of ruby, topaz, diamond, beryl, onyx, jasper, lapis lazuli, turquoise, and emerald. He had settings of gold. This covering may have been a beautiful jeweled robe. Lucifer was an anointed (usually means to be commissioned by and full of the Holy Spirit of God) guardian angel who was on the holy (no evil was present) mountain of God. This is likely a reference to being commissioned to guard God's throne. He walked among "the stones of fire," perhaps a reference to the pavement of sapphire stones under the feet of God on His throne as portrayed in Exodus 24:10. Lucifer was blameless in all his ways and had access to God's garden—Eden (Ezekiel 28:13).

Even though we are not privy to all the details, it is clear that Lucifer was fabulous and held in great trust and honor by God. However, Lucifer let all this majesty, beauty, and power go to his head. Instead of recognizing it to be God's gift and blessing to him, Lucifer started thinking it was all his own doing and became proud in his actions. He thought he could take God's position and usurp His throne.

Ezekiel tells how Lucifer's heart was lifted up because of his beauty and how his splendor caused him to become corrupted in his thinking. And in Isaiah, we are told what God said about Lucifer:

But you said in your heart, "I will ascend to heaven; I will raise my throne above the stars [sons] of God, and I will sit on the mount of assembly in the recesses of the north. I will ascend above the heights of the clouds; I will make myself like the Most High."

—Isa.14:13–14

Yes, Lucifer wanted Daddy's throne. This was the introduction of evil into God's creation—a force never in existence before then. How was God to deal with such rebellion? Sons cannot get away with doing wrong. Correction must come from the Father. Evil left unchecked will only grow and spread. That is exactly what happened. Soon other angels were joining in the rebellion against Father God until a third of all the angels were involved (Revelation 12:4). It was called unrighteousness and sin and corruption.

God, who is totally righteous, holy, and just could not tolerate the presence of such things. The nature of wrongdoing is that punishment and correction must always be administered. In His wrath, God brought a swift end to the rebellion. He kicked Lucifer and his co-conspirators out of heaven, and His Holy Spirit was removed from them. Isaiah 14:11–12 says:

"Your pomp and *the music of your harps have been brought down to Sheol; maggots are spread out* as your bed *beneath you and worms are your covering." How you have fallen from heaven, O star of the morning, son of the dawn!*

In Daniel 8:10, we read how the evil force "grew up to the host of heaven and caused some of the host and some of the stars [sons] to fall to the earth." In Luke 10:18, we see the Lord telling how he watched this event take place. He says, "I was watching Satan fall from heaven like lightning."

Lucifer became Satan (also known as the devil or deviser of evil), and the other rebellious angels became demons when the holiness of God's Spirit left them. They became corrupted by evil and were kicked out of heaven. They became evil spiritual beings that now take their orders from Satan. And we have already noted that spiritual beings are eternal. They became eternally evil.

It was a sad day. There was no other way to deal with unrighteous behavior. We know from our legal system that breaking the law always has a penalty. God was justified and right in His actions. He can never act contrary to what is legally right. It is not in His character. Sadly, these sons could never be redeemed. There was no redemption plan in place for them. Spiritual beings who have made a choice are eternally bound by the choice they have made.

True, there were still two-thirds of the angels who were devoted to God. Their righteousness (right relationship with God) lasts forever. BUT . . . God still wanted more sons in whom He could take delight—sons who would love and trust Him of their own free will. But this same thing could happen all over again.

How could God justify bringing wrath against Satan and angels for their sin but not bringing the same wrath against a new son if he sinned? That wouldn't be fair. It was unthinkable for God to create more sons without a way laid out beforehand to redeem them from evil and wrong choices.

What if they could make the choice to love and trust Him before they were in an unredeemable spiritual state? What if God could make new creatures as sons and make a way to redeem them rather than having to punish them—a way to show mercy to them without compromising His righteous character?

Chapter 5

Enter Man—a New Creature

Before God ever created another being He would have as a son, He put a redemption plan in place that would be enacted if it became necessary. The new plan made a way for God to be exonerated from wrongdoing if He failed to punish sinners. Unlike His former creation, this being would be redeemable, and God would be able to show His mercy without compromising His righteousness.

This new being was called man. Like angels, man was created an eternal creature. However, man was different from the first creation. Man's design would make him redeemable. Unlike angels, man has a natural, physical body of flesh and blood. He also has a spiritual component with a spirit living in his body. Along with a body and a spirit, God put in man a soul for thinking, feeling, and making choices. This makeup allowed man freedom to decide whether he would choose to love and obey God or to be his own god as Satan had done. God did not want robots for His sons. If man chose to love and obey God, the spiritual side of man would prevail, but if not, the natural side would, and punishment would come. The decision would affect not only the man, but also all his offspring.

When God made man, he was perfect. He was a son of God with God's Spirit living in him. The Holy Spirit controlled man's spiritual side, and man walked with God in the world God prepared for him. Man didn't know rebellion or evil, but God knew that these forces and choices existed and warned man not to be fooled. So, before God's adversary, the devil, had a chance to corrupt this new being, the redemption plan was laid out and put in place—something totally new and different that Satan didn't understand. It involved blood.

Before we explore this amazing plan God prepared, let's look at what happened to the first man God created.

God prepared a beautiful physical world for his creation to live in. It had every good thing man needed—plants, animals, light, water, air, land, and most importantly, fellowship with God. He created Adam and breathed His own Holy Spirit into him, full of the life of God, making Adam a son of God. Then He created Eve from Adam's own side for companionship. God walked with them every day in a lovely garden. It was a joyful, delightful place, full of light and goodness. Nothing was corrupt or evil, and they could live in that state forever unless . . .

God warned them that evil did exist. He told them not to eat of the tree of the knowledge of good and evil. They already had knowledge of everything good and could only be harmed by knowing evil. If they did choose evil by disobeying God's command, they would die. The wonderful Holy Spirit that was in them, giving them life and making them sons of God, would depart from them because God's Holy Spirit simply cannot cohabitate with sin. The flesh side of their being would take over, and their days would be limited before their bodies died. Their fellowship with God would be broken. Void of the Spirit, they would no longer be sons of God.

The thought of this delighted Satan to no end, so he set up a plan to sabotage God's creation as he had done with the angels he had previously led into rebellion. One day, Satan invited himself into the lovely garden that God had given Adam and Eve and started a conversation with them. He put doubt into their minds about God's goodness and convinced them that God had lied to them. (In case you haven't noticed, the devil is telling us the same things today.) He tricked Adam and Eve into eating from the tree of the knowledge of good and evil. Once they did, Adam and Eve immediately lost God's Spirit and everything God had given them. They were no longer sons of God. Satan then owned them and became their master.

Chapter 6

The Redemption Plan Is Rolled Out

B ut Satan didn't anticipate what God had planned. This was a secret plan, a mystery that God guarded and kept from Satan so that he could not thwart it. The plan would be revealed to everyone after it had been fully executed centuries later. In 1 Corinthians, the apostle Paul tells how after the cross, God unveiled His secret plan. The mystery of redemption would no longer be hidden but was out in the open for everyone:

> *We speak God's hidden wisdom in a mystery, a wisdom God predestined before the ages for our glory. None of the rulers of this age knew this wisdom, for if they had known it, they would not have crucified the Lord of glory.*
> 1 Cor. 2:7–8 HCSB

And again, Paul states this in Ephesians:

> *How that by revelation he made known unto me the mystery . . . which in other ages was not made known unto the sons of men, as it is now revealed unto his holy apostles and prophets by the Spirit.*
> —Eph. 3:3,5 KJV

Yes, unlike Satan, these human creatures were redeemable. They were stripped of the Holy Spirit, and their own spirits were dead. Thankfully, they were in a corrupted flesh state but not stuck permanently in an evil spiritual state like Satan.

The Holy Spirit had departed from man, but God would provide a new way for man to once again believe and trust Him so that the Holy Spirit could return to live in man and restore him to sonship. God would use flesh and blood that He had created to redeem people. By making man flesh and blood, sin would be confined to the flesh part of man's being where it would be permanently condemned and put to death: "God . . . condemned sin in the flesh" (Romans 8:3). Once executed, the plan would be a permanent fix for those who chose it. The redeemed could ultimately discard the sinful flesh and be transformed into holy spiritual beings.

God's marvelous plan would show everyone, especially the devil, God's righteousness in a new way. God would be righteous when showing mercy instead of wrath to sinful people. A Redeemer's blood would make the difference. "But now, apart from the law, God's righteousness has been revealed—attested by the Law and the Prophets" (Romans 3:21 HCSB).

Blood is a key component for redemption. Let's learn more about its use to save us. We have said earlier that spiritual beings do not have flesh and blood. It is foreign ground to them, but that is the way God made them. As stated earlier, man is different. He has blood running through his veins, and his blood is life to him. Both blood and life and how they interact are mysterious to us. The Bible sheds more light on this mystery. God tells us in Leviticus 17:11 that "the life of the flesh is in the blood." Leviticus 17:14 says, "For *as for the* life of all flesh, its blood is *identified* with its life. . . . 'for the life of all flesh is its blood.'" Blood is not life, but it carries life. This is true for both man and beast.

God made man from the ground—the natural, physical substances of this planet that give man the natural side of his makeup, his body. God then breathed His breath (His own spiritual life) into the man to give man his spiritual makeup. The spirit, which is the life, is held in and carried by the blood of the person. Not only does the blood carry the spirit of the person, but it was made to carry God's Spirit as well. Life is spiritual, but God created the blood to carry it, and the natural and the spiritual meet in it.

Since blood carries life, it is very valuable. A person cannot live without blood. A person can bleed to death. When the blood leaves the body, so does the spirit of life, and a person ceases to breathe. We have devised ways for infusing blood into people when they are injured or sick. We store blood in blood banks to transfuse it into those who need it. Even the term *blood banks* shows how valuable blood is, and we talk about giving the gift of life by donating one's blood. Without good, healthy blood, the body declines quickly or dies.

God intentionally made blood this way with immeasurable value for life. To God, blood's qualities make it a currency for purchasing life, for buying man back.

In the book of Romans, chapter 6, verse 23, God says that "the wages of sin is death." Death is the penalty for disobeying God. Adam and Eve's sin brought them into a state of death. Sin entered their hearts, tainted their blood, and spread throughout their bodies with every heartbeat.

We cannot stress enough that God's Spirit will not cohabitate with sin. The Holy Spirit went out of them immediately, and their spiritual side died. Their natural bodies would follow with physical death. When Adam and Eve sinned, all the earthly creation became subject to death and decay along with them. Plants and animals died and decayed. Their children and all descendants of Adam and Eve died through the centuries. It all became futile: "For the creation was subjected to futility, not willingly, but because of Him who subjected it" (Romans 8:20). The one sin committed by Adam and Eve made everyone subject to the penalty. It became a class action judgment, and a blanket solution had to be enacted for all. We can almost hear Satan screaming in the background: "Kill them; disown them like you did me!"

So, what does the Bible tell us about redemption and blood's role in it? First, we read in Psalm 49:7–8 that "No man can by any means redeem *his* brother or give to God a ransom for him—for the redemption of his soul is costly." There is no cheap fix for man's rebellion. Man is powerless to save himself. His blood has become contaminated by sin, and he has lost his spiritual connection with God. Just the natural body, void of the Holy Spirit is left. Only a transfusion of holy, life-giving blood, capable of carrying the Holy Spirit, can bring man's spirit to life again and reconnect him to God. But where is this holy blood to come from? All mankind is infected and perverted.

Hebrews 9:22 says, "And according to the Law, *one may* almost *say*, all things are cleansed with blood, and without shedding of blood there is no forgiveness." The Bible also tells us that to redeem a life from sin's penalty, another life must be given to pay for it. In Exodus 21:23, we read that under the law when someone was murdered, the following action was to take place, "But if there is *any further* injury, then you shall appoint *as a penalty* life for life." Life given for life as a penalty.

So shed blood addresses several issues. First, it is required as a penalty for sin. Second, sinless blood can cover sins. Third, holy, sinless human blood can cover, cleanse, and forgive sins. The sinless blood of the Redeemer would do all these things plus carry the Holy Spirit.

For redemption, it can't be just anyone's blood. Sinful blood cannot redeem sinful man. God's plan was to send One with sinless blood to restore what mankind lost. A class action failure that brought judgment to all people required a class action solution that would clear all people. He told Adam and Eve beforehand that this would happen and that this Person would be the Savior of the world (Genesis 3:14–15). But until the Savior came, a temporary stopgap would be used to postpone immediate sentencing of Adam and Eve for their crime.

Chapter 7

A Temporary Plan

There were other creatures living on earth who had not sinned like Adam and Eve—the dear animals that were companions of Adam and Eve. It was true that because of Adam and Eve's sin, the animals too were subject to death and decay, but they were innocent, and their blood was not contaminated. God loved mankind, but His holy eyes could not look upon peoples' sin without the same righteous wrath He had shown toward Satan. But if God could legally and righteously cover their sin with innocent blood so as not to see it, to overlook it, He could temporarily refrain from punishing Adam and Eve and show mercy.

We have already said that the life of a creature is in its blood. Since the penalty of death is required for sin, blood must be shed, and a life must be given to pay for sin—a life for a life. Animal blood is not the same type as human blood. It cannot redeem people. However, God decided that an animal's blood could be shed to temporarily cover the sin of man. The sin would not be forgiven, but rather the sin would be covered as with a blanket, hiding the sin from God's eyes. True, it would only be a temporary thing holding back judgment because sinless human blood is required for mankind's forgiveness and for restoring the Holy Spirit into people. An animal's blood could not blot out the sin, clear man's guilt, or permanently restore life to Adam and Eve. But with valuable, innocent blood being given, at least God could hold back for a period of time from executing deserved judgment against mankind.

So, the first thing God did to bring a measure of restoration after the horrid incident when Adam and Eve sinned was to make a blood covering for Adam and Eve. Adam and Eve knew their sin had exposed them and made them guilty, so they tried to cover themselves with a garment of fig leaves to hide their sin. Their own efforts just weren't sufficient to repair the damage. God, in His love and mercy toward Adam and Eve, stepped in and killed animals and covered the pair with the blood from these animals, giving them garments of skin. The Bible calls this blood covering an atonement. A fig leaf was not adequate to make them acceptable to God. He could see right through it. Only blood makes atonement for the soul. The legal requirement of blood being shed had been met. And Satan could not point a finger at God and say, "Unfair; not right!" Be reminded, God's character is always good and right and above blame. God was acting righteously in delaying judgment because blood had been offered to cover sin.

Covering sin with innocent blood to delay judgment and condemnation became the required practice for centuries until the promised redemption would come. We are going to look at some additional enactments of this requirement.

Cain and Abel

Adam and Eve no longer had access to the beautiful Garden of Eden where they once lived. They had to work hard, and they knew their bodies would one day return to the ground. But in the meantime, they began life as we know it. They had children and experienced limited access to God on a physical level. The Lord made it clear to them that to be acceptable before Him, an offering of blood was always necessary and legally required.

The first two children born to Adam and Eve were named Cain and Abel. One day the two brothers brought an offering to God. Cain was a farmer, and Abel was a shepherd. Cain brought an offering of vegetables to God, while Abel killed one of his best animals and brought the blood to God. God did not accept the "fig leaf" offering of Cain but was satisfied with Abel's blood offering. Our own efforts to pay for sin and make us right with God just aren't good enough. We must bring what is required by the law. The legal requirement is blood.

Cain was angry with God and jealous of his brother, Abel. Cain's anger led him to murder his brother, compounding his sin and bringing harsh consequences.

Job

The book of Job is the oldest book in the Bible. From the earliest time, Satan was intent on destroying man, God's wonderful creation. Job was an individual who believed God and was focused on obeying Him. Satan came before God's judgment seat one day to accuse Job. He told God that Job would deny Him if tested. God declared that Job was right with Him, so we know that blood had been involved somewhere. In fact, in Job 1:5, we are told that the regular practice of Job was to offer sacrifices for all his family in the event that they had sinned. Yes, they were covered by blood and in right standing with God.

At any rate, Satan challenged God saying that Job would curse God to His face if enough trouble came Job's way. To prove Job's loving trust, God gave Satan permission to test Job with many trials. Job remained true to God through it all. Even though Job did not understand what was going on and wanted to die in the midst of all the trouble, he kept believing that God was righteous and good. Three friends came along to counsel Job, but they only added to Job's sorrow. Job did not understand why he had experienced so much trouble as a person who believed God, but he knew God was good and faithful. He knew he was right with God and did not believe God was punishing him for his sin. Job's confession was that God would send a Redeemer at some point in the future.

Job's three friends were unable to prove Job's problems had been brought on him by his own sin. Toward the end of the book, a fourth individual shows up in the narrative, Elihu. Elihu continues to accuse Job and is angry that Job's three friends have not been able to refute Job's claims of innocence. There is just one accuser of man, and that is Satan. It appears that Satan used Elihu to accuse Job. Even to the end of the testing, Satan accused Job through the character of Elihu. It is possible that Satan incarnated or disguised himself as Elihu. At the very least, Satan's evil spirit worked through Elihu.

We are warned in 2 Corinthians 11:14, "No wonder, for even Satan disguises himself as an angel of light." Therefore, we are instructed in 1 John 4:1 as follows: "Beloved, do not believe every spirit, but test the spirits to see whether they are from God, because many false prophets have gone out into the world."

As we near the end of the book, Job has a personal encounter with God, and God ends the whole ordeal, vindicating Job. God tells Job's three friends that they had not spoken correctly about His good character as Job had. God tells the three friends that they should offer a blood covering for themselves and have Job pray for them. We can only assume the friends needed their sin covered. Elihu strangely disappears from the dialogue, having lost this particular case, and Job is restored by God from his tragic circumstances. Thank you, God, that Job trusted you even though he had very little revelation.

Noah

As time went on, the number of people increased on the earth. Ungodly people also increased. Satan continued to have his hand in things, since he owned the human race. Only the offering of innocent blood was able to limit his actions. As people increased and beautiful women were born to men, the devil saw further opportunity to thwart God's plan for mankind. Satan thought that if he could further corrupt the makeup of man, God would not have the sons He wanted.

As mentioned earlier, sons of God are created by divine, specific acts of God and have a spiritual existence. The only spiritual beings at the time of Noah were either holy angels or fallen, demonic angels. Adam and Eve had started out as spiritual beings and sons of God. But their sin changed that. Man, after his fall, was in a totally physical state. His spirit was dead.

In Genesis 6:1–2, we see the sons of God getting involved with man:

> *Now it came about, when men began to multiply on the face of the land, and daughters were born to them, that the sons of God saw that the daughters of men were beautiful; and they took wives for themselves, whomever they chose.*

Once again, Satan led a rebellion to further corrupt man. Angels are spiritual beings, but, with the permission of God, they can take on a physical body for an earthly assignment. Obviously, without God's permission, Satan prompted the sons of God to leave their first spiritual estate and take on a human state (Jude 6–7) so they could intermarry with human women to produce a distorted creature. We do not know whether the sons of God were additional holy angels who were tempted to do this or whether this involved angels who had already fallen and become demonic. But it appears to be the latter since the name for them in Genesis 6:4 is Nephilim (rendered *Giants*), which means "the fallen one" in Hebrew.[2] The result is seen in Genesis 6:4:

> *The Nephilim were on the earth in those days, and also afterward, when the sons of God came in to the daughters of men, and they bore children to them. Those were the mighty men who were of old, men of renown.*

---

2. *The New Strong's Exhaustive Concordance of the Bible*, "Strong's 5303, Nephilim."

The Nephilim were giants, distorted men, half human and half supernatural, and very wicked. Genesis 6:5–6 describes God's response:

> *Then the LORD saw that the wickedness of man was great on the earth, and that every intent of the thoughts of his heart was only evil continually. The LORD was sorry that He had made man on the earth, and He was grieved in His heart.*

God decided to wipe out His entire earthly creation. Except for one man. . . . Thank you, God, for Noah.

Noah was a man who wanted to do what was right. God called him "righteous" or right with him. And we know there is only one way for sinful man to be right with God— by blood. Noah obviously had a relationship with God. Was there still hope for God to have the holy sons He wanted? God told Noah to build an ark, a special boat to hold and save a remnant of His creation from the coming destruction. God would send a flood of water to wipe out all the rest of His creation and start over again. Time was given—more than 100 years—for people to change their minds and get on board. In the end, though, only Noah and his family—eight souls—believed God and were saved from the flood that covered all the earth. So, we see an important dynamic at work: trust. It takes faith to trust what God has said and to act on it.

The flood came, all was wiped out, and only Noah and his family and the animals God instructed Noah to take along on the ark were saved. When the flood subsided and they finally came out of the ark, the first thing Noah did was to give a blood offering to God. Many times, we hear how the animals came on the ark two by two. But the Bible tells us in Genesis 7:2 that Noah took seven of every clean animal on the ark but only two of every unclean animal. Noah took from each of the clean animals and made an offering to God. Once again, man's sin was covered by blood, and God could be merciful to him. God swore He would never again destroy every living thing as

He had done, even though the intent of man in his unredeemed state is evil from his youth. God placed the rainbow in the sky as a sign of that promise.

Satan's plans were thwarted. The rebellious, demonic sons who had been involved in the latest fiasco were locked up for good until the final judgment as recorded in Jude 6: "And angels who did not keep their own domain, but abandoned their proper abode, He has kept in eternal bonds under darkness for the judgment of the great day."

Abraham

Many years passed after the time of Noah. God wanted to move His redemption plan for mankind forward. He looked throughout the earth to find someone who could help further that plan—someone who would trust Him and cooperate with Him so that a Redeemer could come to the earth for mankind. God found such a man in Abraham. God talked with Abraham and told him that He wanted to separate Abraham from the rest of the "pack." Abraham was told to leave his country and go to a new land that God would show him. There God would establish him and make him into the father of a new people from whom a Redeemer could come. Abraham believed God and obeyed Him. When Abraham got to Canaan, God appeared to Abraham and promised to give the land to him and his descendants. Abraham responded to God by offering blood sacrifices. Yes, the man of God knows what it takes to cover sins.

There was just one little problem. Abraham was old. His wife Sarah was old. And they had no children. How could they possibly have any descendants—I mean, a whole nation? He was 75, going on 100! But God said so, and Abraham believed Him:

> *Then behold, the word of the LORD came to him, saying, "This man will not be your heir; but one who shall come forth from your own body, he shall be your heir." And He took him outside and said, "Now look toward the heavens,*

and count the stars, if you are able to count them." And He said to him, "So shall your descendants be." Then he believed in the LORD; and He reckoned it to him as righteousness.

—Gen. 15:4–6

God made the promise, Abraham believed Him, and the whole agreement was sealed with a blood offering. It was a legal covenant (contract) filed in heaven (Genesis 15:7–21).

Time passed and still no son. Abraham was 99 and Sarah was 89. They found themselves in a lot of trouble trying to "help" God make things happen. We won't go into that now. But the time was ripe, and God once again appeared to Abraham and told him that by the next year, Sarah would have a son. Soon Sarah was pregnant; the year passed, and Isaac was born to Abraham and Sarah, now 100 and 90, respectively. What joy! Faith and blood had met, and God did the miraculous. From this child, a nation would grow, and from that nation, a Redeemer would come into the world to buy back sinners.

But first, God wanted to test his plan a little more before its full execution. Would anyone really believe that a man could give his blood for people's sins and rise again from death? God put the test to Abraham. Isaac had grown into a young man and was the joy of his father's heart. God said to Abraham, "Take now your son, your only son, whom you love, Isaac, and go to the land of Moriah, and offer him there as a burnt offering on one of the mountains of which I will tell you" (Genesis 22:2).

How could this be? God said that this son would produce innumerable offspring. He was a miraculous child of promise. God promised to bless the whole world through him. This didn't make any sense. But God said it, so there must be more to it. The scripture says, "He [Abraham] considered that God is able to raise *people* even from the dead" (Hebrews 11:19).

So, Abraham saddled his donkey and took the lad as God had told him to present him as an offering. Isaac asked his dad where the animal was for the offering, and Abraham told him that God would provide the lamb. They came to the place where the sacrifice would be given. Abraham raised the knife to kill his son. But wait! Just when Abraham raised the knife to offer Isaac, God called out to him from heaven and said, "Abraham, Abraham! . . . Do not stretch out your hand against the lad, and do nothing to him; for now I know that you fear God, since you have not withheld your son, your only son, from Me" (Genesis 22:11–12).

God then provided a ram that was standing nearby with its horns caught in a thicket for the needed offering. Yes, someone really did believe God. God was not going to put an end to His plan of providing a nation from which a Savior would come. God could have ended the whole thing right there with Isaac. It would have saved Him a whole lot of pain, but because of His love for us, He didn't. God would continue to let the blood of animals fulfill the legal requirement of covering sin until He would give His own Son who would come through the lineage of Abraham to pay the full penalty of sin once and for all.

Thank you, God, that Abraham trusted and obeyed you. He became the father of faith for all of us who walk in faith like he did—a father of a large group of people and a blessing to many nations.

Abraham lived in Canaan, the land God gave to him and his descendants. His son Isaac had children, who had their own stories. Abraham's grandson Jacob had twelve children. And from these children would come a nation, from whom the promised Redeemer would come. Jacob had an encounter with God at which time God changed Jacob's name to Israel, and the nation God would establish through him would be known as Israel.

Joseph

During Jacob's life, a widespread famine took place in the land where Jacob lived—the land of Canaan that was home to his grandpa and dad—the land that would become Israel. Through a series of events, Jacob and his sons moved to Egypt to be saved from starvation.

One of Jacob's twelve sons was named Joseph. Joseph was a dreamer after God's heart. He dreamed that God had a great purpose for him and that he would rule over his brothers and his father as part of that purpose. Of course, sharing that vision only made his brothers angry and jealous. In their hatred, Joseph's brothers planned to kill him and act as if his death was a tragic incident that they had nothing to do with. One of the brothers had somewhat of a conscience and convinced the rest to spare Joseph's life. Instead of killing him, they threw him in a pit, took his clothing, and put blood on it to look like a wild animal had attacked Joseph. Then they showed the coat to their father. Of course, Jacob thought Joseph was dead. Instead, when a merchant caravan headed to Egypt came near the pit, Joseph's brothers sold him as a slave to the traders. Joseph ended up in Egypt as a slave.

Joseph's brothers had evil intentions, but God had different plans. It was just the beginning of the fulfillment of Joseph's dreams. God was with Joseph and gave him wisdom and favor with his masters. Everything was going well until he was falsely accused by his owner of misconduct and landed in jail. But even there, he gained favor with the prison wardens. Joseph's dreams once again came to life. The Pharaoh had a dream that couldn't be explained, and it bothered him. Both the prison guards and those who had been prisoners with Joseph were well aware of the ability God had given Joseph to interpret dreams. Word got to Pharaoh, and he sent for Joseph in hope of learning the meaning of his dreams.

God showed Joseph that Pharaoh's dreams foretold of a devastating famine that would cover much of the world. There would be abundant harvests for seven years, followed by seven years of famine. Joseph advised Pharaoh to put aside part of the abundance of the first seven years as a provision for the years of famine. Pharaoh put Joseph in charge of implementing his own advice and made him ruler over all the land of Egypt, second only to Pharaoh.

God had sent Joseph ahead of His people to Egypt to save them from famine and death. During the famine, Joseph's brothers came to Egypt in search of food. It was quite a humbling experience when they found Joseph in charge of the Pharaoh's domain. After Joseph's father, Jacob, and brothers were reunited with Joseph, the family moved to Egypt for their preservation. Jacob (now known as Israel) would eat from Joseph's table. Once again, the devil's attempts to stop God's plans to redeem man were thwarted. A nation from which the Redeemer would come would be established.

Moses

The Israelites had favor with the Pharaoh, and their descendants stayed in Egypt for 400 years. During that time, the people multiplied and grew into the millions. Over the centuries, they lost favor with the Pharaohs and became enslaved to them. During Abraham's life, God had told him this would happen, but that He would send a deliverer to bring the people out of slavery, return them to Canaan, and make them into a nation.

Near the end of the 400 years in Egypt, a beautiful child named Moses was born. The Pharaoh wanted to destroy the babies that were born to the sons of Israel because he feared that the Israelites were becoming too powerful and would rebel against the Egyptians. To save Moses from the Pharaoh's murderous plans, Moses's parents tried to hide Moses from the Egyptians, but it became too difficult. So, his parents devised a plan to abandon him in a basket in the reeds of the Nile River where the Pharaoh's daughter came to bathe in hope that she would find him and take him in. The plan worked. She had pity on the baby and took him in as her own, raising him in the palace. Thus, Moses was raised in the ways and wisdom of royalty—very important skills needed to lead a people and a nation.

At the age of forty, after living in the royal palace his entire life, Moses ended up in trouble with the Pharaoh, fled Egypt, and made his home in the land of Midian. Moses spent another forty years in the wilderness, being a shepherd and learning the skills of survival in the desert. The time drew near when God would send him back to Egypt to lead the Israelites out of Egypt back to the land of Canaan from which they came. You can read the whole story in Exodus chapters 1–7.

While Moses was living in Midian, he encountered God in a dramatic way. God told Moses to return to Egypt because God had chosen him to deliver the Israelites from their slavery to Pharaoh. God instructed Moses to bring them back to Canaan, where God would fulfill his promises to Abraham by making them into a nation that would bless all mankind. God directed Moses to meet with his brother, Aaron, upon arriving in Egypt. Aaron would become a helper to Moses in fulfilling the plan God had for the sons of Israel.

Moses's assignment was to confront Pharaoh and demand the release of the Israelites. Pharaoh was not one to easily roll over and give in. But Moses became God's spokesman, and his words were backed up with mighty demonstrations of God's power. Moses came to Pharaoh and told him to release the sons of Israel from their slavery to him so they could depart from Egypt. The Pharaoh would have nothing to do with the directive Moses delivered from God. So, God sent a series of ten plagues against Pharaoh and his country to convince him. Pharaoh resisted, and much harm was done to his land, until God sent one final plague to convince Pharaoh and judge him for his lack of compliance.

God announced this final plague to Pharaoh through Moses.

> *Moses said, "Thus says the LORD, 'About midnight I am going out into the midst of Egypt, and all the firstborn in the land of Egypt shall die, from the firstborn of the Pharaoh who sits on his throne, even to the firstborn of the slave girl who is behind the millstones; all the firstborn of the cattle as well. Moreover, there shall be a great cry in all the land of Egypt, such as there has not been before and such as shall*

never be again. But against any of the sons of Israel a dog will not even bark, whether against man or beast, that you may understand how the LORD makes a distinction between Egypt and Israel."

—Exod. 11:4–7

God gave Moses specific instructions to protect the Israelites from this last plague that was coming against the land of Egypt so that they would not be subject to the same wrath being shown to the Egyptians. Once again, blood was involved. A death angel would come through the land and kill all the firstborn of man and animal, unless a household believed God and did what God told them.

Now the LORD said to Moses and Aaron in the land of Egypt, "This month shall be the beginning of months for you; it is to be the first month of the year to you. Speak to all the congregation of Israel, saying, 'On the tenth of this month they are each one to take a lamb for themselves, according to their fathers' households, a lamb for each household. Now if the household is too small for a lamb, then he and his neighbor nearest to his house are to take one according to the number of persons in them; according to what each man should eat, you are to divide the lamb. Your lamb shall be an unblemished male a year old; you may take it from the sheep or from the goats. You shall keep it until the fourteenth day of the same month, then the whole assembly of the congregation of Israel is to kill it at twilight. Moreover, they shall take some of the blood and put it on the two doorposts and on the lintel of the houses in which they eat it. They shall eat the flesh that same night, roasted with fire, and they shall eat it with unleavened bread and bitter herbs. Do not eat any of it raw or boiled at all with water, but rather roasted with fire, both its head and its legs along

with its entrails. And you shall not leave any of it over until morning, but whatever is left of it until morning, you shall burn with fire. Now you shall eat it in this manner: with *your loins girded, your sandals on your feet, and your staff in your hand; and you shall eat it in haste—it is the LORD's Passover. For I will go through the land of Egypt on that night, and will strike down all the firstborn in the land of Egypt, both man and beast; and against all the gods of Egypt I will execute judgments—I am the LORD. The blood shall be a sign for you on the houses where you live; and when I see the blood I will pass over you, and no plague will befall you to destroy you when I strike the land of Egypt.'"*
—Exod. 12:1–13

Every family that did what God said and put the blood from the lamb over and on the sides of the door to their house was protected from this last plague of death. They were saved from death as long as they stayed inside their house until morning so that they were under the protection of the blood covering until the destroyer passed by. But all the Egyptians, without this blood covering, experienced the penalty of sin—death. So, we see once again, blood and faith in the shed blood allowed God to pass over sin for those who believed Him.

Chapter 8
A New Dimension to the Plan—How to Grow and Rule a Nation

At last, Pharaoh allowed the sons of Israel to leave Egypt. God gave the Israelites favor with their Egyptian neighbors. He told them to ask the Egyptians to give them articles of silver, gold, and clothing upon their departure. The Israelites left Egypt with great spoil, including large herds of livestock.

Even after all the judgment that God executed against him, Pharaoh's heart hardened, and he chased after the Israelites to destroy them and bring them back to Egypt. But God had a different plan. He was bringing His people back to Canaan to fulfill the promises He made to Abraham, Isaac, and Jacob centuries earlier. Pharaoh and his army pursued Israel to the Red Sea. God parted the waters of the Red Sea for the Israelites to escape and pass through on dry ground. When the Egyptians followed them, God allowed the waters to crash back over these enemies, never again to be seen by the Israelites.

Yes, the Israelites had become a company of millions. This was a new nation for God's purpose. They had been slaves. Now they were a people with a God-given destiny and a lot to learn.

Giving of the Law

The Israelites were free at last. But freedom also requires structure. Everyone doesn't automatically do what is right. If that were the case, Adam and Eve wouldn't have sinned in the first place, and the world wouldn't be in such a mess. God had set up a temporary measure to cover sin if man would trust and obey God by offering an animal's blood, but it didn't change man's heart or rein him in from bad behavior. It was time to set some dos and don'ts. If you don't have some rules, you can't tell someone they are breaking them and that there are consequences. They can't be held accountable.

So, the law was given so that everyone would become accountable for their actions. Romans 5:13 says, "For until the Law sin was in the world, but sin is not imputed when there is no law." In Romans 7:7, the apostle Paul says, "I would not have come to know sin except through the Law; for I would not have known about coveting if the Law had not said, 'YOU SHALL NOT COVET.'"

God led Moses and the sons of Israel through the wilderness on their way back to Canaan. In the third month after the Israelites left Egypt, God took them to Mount Sinai where He gave them the laws that would govern their nation. Moses went up on the mountain to meet with God for forty days. God appeared to Moses and gave him His law. This included the Ten Commandments and all the rules pertaining to worship, civil and criminal law, property rights, marriage and family law, Sabbath and holiday regulations, and regulations related to conquering and acquiring the land for their new nation. He gave Moses the architectural plans for building a place of worship, a portable tent to go with them as they journeyed to the new land.

God set up the Levitical priesthood and leadership for administering His law and governing the people. The people were grouped along ancestral lines—twelve tribes descending from the twelve sons of Jacob. Moses and Aaron were from the tribe descended from Levi. God set the entire tribe of Levi apart to serve as priests for administering the worship, and God chose Aaron to be the high priest. His sons and their descending sons would hold the high priest office down through the centuries.

God told the sons of Israel that He would bless them if they agreed to keep His laws and obey Him. Good consequences would come if they obeyed the laws. Their crops, families, and all they did would prosper. Dreadful consequences would happen to them if they disobeyed the laws. Great destruction, loss, and harm would come to their families and country. This judgment became known as the "Curse of the Law." You can read all the blessings and curses in Deuteronomy 28. The Israelites agreed to obey the Law, but it wasn't long before that decision was put to the test. And they failed that test miserably. God was exasperated and angry. He wanted to destroy them all. Except for Moses stepping in and imploring God to relent, all would have been destroyed.

God's law is perfect and good, but people aren't. The law only points out our shortcomings and our need for a changed heart and someone to save us from our inability to live up to its standards. A law doesn't require faith, just obedience—do it whether you believe it or not or suffer the consequences. A law does not engage the heart; it just places a burden of obligation to perform. Romans 3:23 points out our shortcoming, saying, "For all have sinned and fall short of the glory of God."

Thankfully, this is not the end of the story. God has provided something better because God wants to engage our hearts with Him in faith and in trust.

It wasn't an overnight thing for the people to learn to trust and obey their God. They ended up spending forty years in wilderness wandering until all but two of the original adult people who had left Egypt died as a consequence of their disobedience. It was their sons and daughters who eventually made it to the land of promise. During their time in the wilderness, they learned more about their God and what He expected as He accompanied them on their journey. The

Israelites built the worship tabernacle and learned how to worship God. They saw the miraculous power of God and learned of His goodness. They learned how to put His laws into practice. Little by little, God revealed Himself to them and allowed them to see His glory, but never without offering blood. Yes, a Savior was still needed and promised.

National Holidays

All countries have national holidays of significant meaning and importance. Israel is no exception. The Jewish people celebrate nine feasts altogether throughout the year, all memorializing important events. The feasts were meant to be visual portrayals of important spiritual truths God wanted to teach His people so that they would understand what the promised Redeemer would accomplish by His coming.

The Passover

The first feast God put into practice was the Passover. The Israelites were to celebrate the Passover every year with the sacrifice of a lamb and a meal patterned after the first Passover they experienced on the night they left Egypt. It is a perpetual memorial of what God did when He passed over their sin because of the shed blood of the lamb and delivered them from Egyptian bondage. The Passover is also a prophetic picture of what the Redeemer would accomplish in freeing people from slavery to the devil by the sacrifice of His blood. God used precious blood to cover their sins and relent from judgment on the first Passover and would do so again with the Redeemer's blood.

Day of Atonement

One feast of significant importance God commanded the Israelites to observe was the Day of Atonement. The Israelites had left Egypt and were in the desert traveling toward Canaan. Moses had received the Law from God on Mt. Sinai. Instructions had been given for building the worship tabernacle[3] and for how the people were to conduct the worship, along with how to celebrate the special holy days.

God designed the tabernacle in a very special way. The tabernacle, being portable, was moved with the people as they made their journey through the desert to the promised land. God designed it to be a holy place where He could have contact with His people. The tabernacle was frequently referred to as "the tent of meeting"—a place of encounter between God and His people. But man's sin was an ongoing problem, preventing man from coming into God's presence. Only blood could cover sin, and man could not come into God's presence without it. The tabernacle was specifically designed to make this possible. The Most Holy Place was where the meeting would take place. This was an inner room that was veiled off from the outside. Before one could get to that room, there were other areas to pass through and specific actions that had to take place.

The outer courtyard of the tabernacle was about 150 feet long by 75 feet wide. A bronze altar stood in the courtyard where the priests made animal sacrifices for the blood offering for covering man's sins. The courtyard also housed a basin filled with water where the priests washed themselves before entering the tent.

The tabernacle itself, measuring approximately 15 feet by 45 feet, was divided into two sections or rooms. The outer room was known as the Holy Place and was furnished with an altar where incense was burned, a lampstand with seven branches, and a table of showbread (a symbol of God's presence).

The inner room was called the Most Holy Place or Holy of Holies. It was separated from the outer room by a thick veil. Just one item furnished this room, the Ark of the Covenant. The Ark was a gold-covered wooden box that held the stone tablets on which

---

3. *New American Standard Bible, The New Open Bible Study Edition* (Nashville, TN: Thomas Nelson Publishers, 1990), *s.v.* "The Tabernacle," 112.

the Ten Commandments (the covenant between God and man) had been written, a jar of manna (a special God-given food that sustained the Israelites in the desert), and a rod used by Aaron that God caused to supernaturally bud.

The Ark had a gold-clad lid to cover and close it. This lid was known as the mercy seat. Upon this lid, two cherubim, fashioned from gold, faced each other. It was at the mercy seat where the encounter with God and man took place. Only the high priest could take part in this meeting, and just one time a year on the Day of Atonement, but never without blood.

Each year on the Day of Atonement, Aaron met God in the Most Holy Place at the mercy seat, where God's presence descended in a cloud. Specific steps were taken to cover both Aaron's sin and the people's sin, so that Aaron would not die in God's sinless presence. We won't go into the detailed requirements found in Leviticus 16, but I will briefly summarize the process.

In the courtyard, Aaron killed the animals for the sacrifice—a bull and a ram. In addition, he took two male goats from the people for a sin offering. He washed himself in the basin and put on holy garments made of linen and patterned by God. He first made atonement for himself (a blood covering for his sins) and then atonement (blood covering) for the people.

The offering of the two goats was especially significant and symbolic in the redemption plan, for it was a portrayal of what the Redeemer would accomplish for us. Aaron set the two male goats before the Lord at the doorway of the tent of meeting. There he cast lots (rolled the dice) for the goats. One lot would go to the Lord, and one lot would be for the scapegoat. The goat for the Lord was sacrificed for a sin offering. Its blood was in payment for the sins of the people.

Before Aaron could enter the Most Holy Place, he had to offer incense on the altar in the Holy Place and then bring the incense in a firepan into the Most Holy Place, along with the blood from the sacrifices.

The blood from the animal sacrifices was brought into the Most Holy Place, and Aaron used a finger to sprinkle blood on the mercy seat and in front of the mercy seat, crying out to God for mercy. The blood covered the sins of the people and Aaron's sins, and it purified the tent of meeting and its furnishings. The pleasing cloud of incense rose from the firepan before the mercy seat, and God met with Aaron. In mercy, God and man met and communed—a foretaste of the sweet fellowship that the coming Redeemer would provide.

After the meeting at the mercy seat, Aaron offered the live goat at the doorway of the tent of meeting. He put his hands on the goat's head, confessing and putting on the goat all the Israelites' sins. Then the goat was sent away alive into the wilderness bearing all the iniquities of the people, never to be seen again.

The offering of the two goats was a vivid picture of what the Redeemer would accomplish. He would give his blood like the first goat to pay for and cover the people's sins; but His sacrifice would go beyond that, bringing mercy and forgiveness forever. And like the second goat, He also would become our scapegoat, standing in our place and carrying our sins away to a place where they would never again be seen.

God gave the Israelites a foretaste of the goodness and mercy of God that mankind was going to experience.

Chapter 9

Show Me Your Glory— the Glory of God

*G*lory is a rather mysterious word. It is hard to put your finger on exactly what it is. People use it all the time to express wonder and excitement. But what does it mean?

We have just reviewed the account of the role that Moses played in the redemption story. Most people have at least a basic familiarity with what took place because of the Passover portrayal they have seen on TV or the movie screen. We have seen enactments of Moses parting the Red Sea and watched the Pharaoh lead the Egyptian army to their death in the Red Sea where they drowned.

While Moses was in the wilderness leading the Israelites to the Promised Land, God traveled with them. God told Moses he had found favor in His sight and that His presence would go with Moses and the Israelites as they journeyed to Canaan. They experienced God's presence by day in a cloud that went before them and at night in a pillar of fire that camped with them. Moses said he would not make the journey unless God went with him, and God granted his request.

Even though Moses had experienced the awesome presence of God, he was not fully satisfied, for he still cried out for more: "Show me your glory!" Obviously, there must be some difference between God's presence and God's glory. But what? What did Moses want?

Then Moses said, "I pray You, show me Your glory!" And He [God] said, "I Myself will make all My goodness pass before you, and will proclaim the name of the LORD before you; and I will be gracious to whom I will be gracious, and will show compassion on whom I will show compassion."

—Exod. 33:18–19

Here, God tells us what glory is. Glory is the revelation or manifestation of the gracious goodness of God's nature and acts. Though subtle in this scripture passage, one thing is missing from the glory and can be inadvertently overlooked. Then comes the dawn: The wrath of God is not there! There is no wrath in the glory. There is no condemnation in the glory. Only God's goodness is revealed in the glory. Glory! What He shows Moses is all His goodness, grace, and compassion. He is telling Moses that He is always good and acts in gracious, compassionate ways to those who believe Him. Glory is the manifestation of *God's righteous goodness* toward blood-bought believers *apart from the judgment of the law.*

Moses was crying out and echoing all mankind's heart to experience God's mercy and compassionate grace apart from judgment and wrath. We want to experience God's loving presence as a Father rather than the stern presence of a wrathful judge. That day was coming when intimacy with God's glory would be available to all believers. But for their time, Moses and the Israelites had only a small taste of what was to come.

Throughout the Old Testament, God had specific commands for the people to observe to experience His glory. God cannot be gracious when sin is present. Sins must be dealt with before God's goodness can be experienced. Only blood can cover sin—a life given to redeem a life. Jesus had not come yet to shed His precious blood to permanently wipe out the consequences of sin. So, a temporary covering of sins by blood had to be provided before God could show His glory (goodness) to the people.

We remember that the Israelites had been told to kill a lamb and put its blood on the doorposts and lintel of the doors at their homes in Egypt prior to the time they left that country. As a judgment on Pharaoh and the Egyptians, the death angel passed through the land of Egypt and killed the firstborn males in the land. When God saw the blood on the doors of the Israelites, their homes were passed over and their firstborn were spared from death. Their faith in the blood saved them and kept the wrath of God from touching them.

In Leviticus, Moses told the people what God said they had to do to quench the wrath and make a way for the glory of the Lord to appear to them:

> *Moses said, "This is the thing which the LORD has commanded you to do, that the glory of the LORD may appear to you." Moses then said to Aaron, "Come near to the altar and offer your sin offering and your burnt offering, that you may make atonement for yourself and for the people; then make the offering for the people, that you may make atonement for them, just as the LORD has commanded." . . . Then Aaron lifted up his hands toward the people and blessed them, and he stepped down after making the sin offering and the burnt offering and the peace offerings. Moses and Aaron went into the tent of meeting. When they came out and blessed the people, the glory of the LORD appeared to all the people. Then fire came out from before the LORD and consumed the burnt offering and the portions of fat on the altar; and when all the people saw it, they shouted and fell on their faces.*
>
> —Lev. 9:6–7, 22–24

As the blood had allowed the Israelites to experience the compassionate goodness of God on the night of the Passover, the blood also allowed them to experience God's glorious goodness in the wilderness. The sacrifice Aaron made atoned for their sins and turned God's wrath away. The glory appeared, the people were awe-struck, and fell to the ground in the presence of God.

God answered Moses's longing cry to experience the glory of God. He went on to fulfill his destiny not only with the presence of God, but also with the encouraging experience of knowing God's goodness and compassion.

Through the centuries, God progressively revealed His gracious nature through the prophets. He told the prophets things about Himself and what He was going to do to save and bless believers. The words He gave the prophets to speak are known as prophecies. In this way, the people heard the words of God and came to know His ways.

Many of the Old Testament prophecies foretold of a way and time when God's glory would be revealed in a greater and more understandable way. In time, God was going to graphically reveal Himself through a person Who would take on the very nature and actions of God. This Person would bring the glory of God (the revelation of God's goodness and compassion) in a way that people could see and experience. Hebrews 1:1–3 tells us:

> *God, after He spoke long ago to the fathers in the prophets in many portions and in many ways, in these last days has spoken to us in His Son, whom He appointed heir of all things, through whom also He made the world. And He is the radiance of His glory and the exact representation of His nature and upholds all things by the word of His power.*

This promised One came in human form as Jesus Christ. Jesus was full of the glory of God and revealed God's goodness to us. Just consider all the kind acts of healing and deliverance He performed for people! Men and women could look at Jesus's actions and see exactly what God is like—a compassionate, loving father.

The apostle John says, "And the Word became flesh, and dwelt among us, and we saw His glory, glory as of the only begotten from the Father, full of grace and truth" (John 1:14). Just looking at Jesus and hearing what He said was like looking directly into the face of God the Father. Jesus showed us what God is like by everything He said and did. He knew God as Father and displayed how God intended the relationship between God and man to be. And God confirmed what Jesus said by working mighty miracles through Him, helping people everywhere Jesus went. Glory to God!

Jesus's blood would cover our sins permanently, allowing the glory of God to come into the lives of all believers. The Word of God says that man will be crowned with glory and honor. That glory is available today for those who have received Jesus's redemption for them. Today, it is the believer's privilege and responsibility to shine forth God's goodness and character to those around him through the same Spirit who lived in Jesus. People should be able to look at believers and see the image of God in them so that they too can come to know the Father. Hebrews puts it this way:

> *WHAT IS MAN, THAT YOU REMEMBER HIM? OR THE SON OF MAN, THAT YOU ARE CONCERNED ABOUT HIM? YOU HAVE MADE HIM FOR A LITTLE WHILE LOWER THAN THE ANGELS; YOU HAVE CROWNED HIM WITH GLORY AND HONOR, AND HAVE APPOINTED HIM OVER THE WORKS OF YOUR HANDS.*
>
> —Heb. 2:6–7

> *For it was fitting for Him, for whom are all things, and through whom are all things, in bringing many sons to glory, to perfect the author of their salvation [Jesus] through sufferings.*
>
> —Heb. 2:10

Jesus suffered and died for us so that we may bear His image and show the glory of God!

Chapter 10

The Law—the Courtroom of God, Legal Covenants God Made

Before we move on to the Israelites entering the Promised Land, let's take a closer look at the legal side of God's interactions with his creation.

God Is the Judge

We can well conclude that heaven has a courtroom and a justice system for ruling the universe. God is the judge in that courtroom and enacts the legal system as He designed it. He does not deviate from what He has set up for Himself or anything under His jurisdiction. First, let's look at some references that confirm that God is the supreme judge. The Bible says:

> *Far be it from You to do such a thing, to slay the righteous with the wicked, so that the righteous and the wicked are treated alike. Far be it from You! Shall not the Judge of all the earth deal justly?*
>
> —Gen. 18:25

May the LORD look upon you and judge you.
—Exod. 5:21

May the LORD, the Judge, judge today between the sons of Israel and the sons of Ammon.
—Judges 11:27

But God is the judge: he putteth down one, and setteth up another.
—Ps. 75:7 KJV

Nature of the Judge

What kind of judge is God? The Bible says God is a righteous and just judge:

And he shall judge the world in righteousness, he shall minister judgment to the people in uprightness.
—Ps. 9:8 KJV

God is not guilty of any wrongdoing when he judges:

Against You—You alone—I have sinned and done this evil in Your sight. So You are right when You pass sentence; You are blameless when You judge.
—Ps. 51:4 HCSB

The Courtroom

There is a courtroom God presides over. His authority is undeniable, and His judgment seat is a throne.

Micaiah said, "Therefore, hear the word of the LORD. I saw the LORD sitting on His throne, and all the host of heaven standing on His right and on His left."
—2 Chron. 18:18

For You have upheld my just cause; You are seated on Your throne as a righteous judge. . . . But the LORD sits enthroned forever; He has established His throne for judgment.
—Ps. 9:4, 7 HCSB

The LORD is in His holy temple; the LORD's throne is in heaven. His eyes watch; He examines everyone.
—Ps. 11:4 HCSB

Then I saw a great white throne and Him who sat upon it, from whose presence earth and heaven fled away, and no place was found for them. And I saw the dead, the great and the small, standing before the throne, and books were opened; and another book was opened, which is the book of life; and the dead were judged from the things which were written in the books, according to their deeds.
—Rev. 20:11–12

The Courtroom in Session

The courtroom of heaven conducts the legal business for the universe. Not only are legal decisions handed down from the Judge, but also legal documents are filed with the court. God has drawn up numerous legal documents for affairs of heaven and earth. Among these documents are contracts, judgments, promissory notes, covenants, and wills. We will examine some of these instruments. They have all been signed by God, and the signature has been written in blood.

A Promissory Note

One of the earliest of documents was a promissory note given to Adam and Eve. It was the promise of a savior for mankind after Adam and Eve sinned. In Genesis 3:15, God says, "I will put hostility between you and the woman, and between your seed and her seed. He will strike your head, and you will strike his heel" (HCSB).

This verse tells of the battle that mankind and his offspring have with the devil and how the devil will constantly be attacking mankind. But He (the Savior) will strike the devil's head and put an end to the devil's work. God made this promise and put it into effect when He covered Adam and Eve with animal skins and covered them with blood. The blood signature was the guarantee of the promise.

The Rainbow Covenant

A covenant is a contract. Covenants are well-known in many parts of the world where civilization is older and often tribal. The covenant is frequently made between a stronger and weaker party. They join together to form a stronger alliance and will come to each other's aid. The parties would rather die than break their agreement. The word *covenant* comes from a word meaning "to cut." The individuals involved make a cut in their skin and mingle their blood, becoming blood brothers. They then exchange gifts with each other and words of promise to stay true to helping each other. Nothing can break this bond.

One of the first covenants God made with mankind was after the flood. Staying under the blood covering, Noah offered the blood of animal sacrifices to God in appreciation and honor of God's salvation for him and his family. God promised to never again destroy His creation with a flood and put the rainbow in the sky as a sign of this covenant—signed in blood and stamped with a rainbow. God always keeps His side of the covenant, even though man may break it. But we are expected to keep our side if we want to have the benefits of the contract.

The Abrahamic Covenant

The Abrahamic Covenant was a contract between God and Abraham that God would give Abraham a son from whom many descendants would come, making Abraham a father of many nations, the father of faith, and the means by which mankind would reinherit the world, which had been lost to the devil.

The covenant was cut when God told Abraham to bring a blood sacrifice of a three-year-old cow, a three-year-old goat, a three-year-old ram, a turtledove, and a young pigeon. Both parties kept their part of the agreement, even when Abraham found it challenging. As a result, all the promises came to pass, and Abraham was counted faithful and righteous with God. God gave Abraham a special stamp of approval—the sign of circumcision, a sign of the faith Abraham had to believe and obey God; this was a blood covering that symbolized that Abraham's sins were covered and that he was acceptable to God.

The Old Covenant of the Law

It was 430 years (Galatians 3:17) after the covenant with Abraham when God drew up the Old Covenant and the Law established by it. The Law was given for specific reasons defined by Scripture. It became the legal system ruling the nation of Israel. The country was a theocracy with laws based on spiritual principles. We must remember that sin had been in the world since Adam and Eve sinned, and death—the consequence of sin—had been experienced by all mankind through the generations. But there had not been a formal, written legal code in place.

However, where there is no law, one cannot be held accountable for breaking the law. If there is no law that says you cannot drive your car over the speed limit, you cannot be held guilty for driving too fast, no matter how unsafe it may be. So, the law was put into effect, and the law made everyone accountable for their actions, and it brought a means of enacting justice:

> *Now we know that whatever the Law says, it speaks to those who are under the Law, so that every mouth may be closed, and all the world may become accountable to God; . . . for through the Law comes the knowledge of sin.*
>
> —Rom. 3:19–20

And in Galatians 3:19, we are told why God added the Law: "Why the Law then? It was added because of transgressions." The Law also makes us aware of our shortcomings and points us to the need of a Redeemer. Galatians 3:24 says, "Therefore the Law has become our tutor *to lead us* to Christ."

The Old Covenant is more frequently known as the Old Testament. We would call it a Last Will and Testament. The *fulfillment* of a will goes into effect upon the death of the maker. But like any will, the *terms* of the Old Covenant were put into effect when God wrote the laws on the tablets of stone and gave them to Moses. The people accepted the terms of the contract, and the covenant was signed and sealed in blood. Animal sacrifice to cover sin became a central part of the worship. Moses read the covenant to the Israelites, and they agreed to its terms. Then Moses sprinkled the blood of the offering on the people and the altar.

There were great blessings for keeping the laws and severe consequences for breaking them. The consequences became known as the Curse of the Law. Disobedience brought sickness, poverty, and harm. Keeping the Law brought health, wealth, and protection. But keeping the Law wasn't easy, and Israel spent a lot of time under the Curse. Oh, for a better way!

The New Covenant

The New Covenant, better known as the New Testament, went into effect when Jesus came to the earth and gave His life for our sins. It replaced the Old Covenant and is the contract that we are operating under now. It is a marvelous contract that we will examine in the rest of this book. It provides for mercy and grace like no other contract that has been drawn up in heaven. It is the epitome of God's redemption plan for man through which the promised Redeemer saves mankind. The New Covenant was cut with the blood of Jesus Christ when He died on the cross. Jesus Himself instituted the memorial of communion to remind us of what He did. In Matthew 26:26–28, we read what Jesus said:

> *While they were eating, Jesus took* some *bread, and after a blessing, He broke* it *and gave* it *to the disciples, and said, "Take, eat; this is My body." And when He had taken a cup and given thanks, He gave* it *to them, saying, "Drink from it, all of you; for this is My blood of the covenant, which is poured out for many for forgiveness of sins."*

This contract has a new set of laws. It establishes the law of the Spirit of Life in Christ Jesus and the law of love for God and other people.

Legal Cases

Legal cases are also tried in heaven's courtroom. We have briefly touched on a few of the cases:

- Lucifer being judged for rebellion and exiled from heaven to become the devil.
- Adam and Eve sinning and being expelled from the Garden of Eden. They received a judgment of death. This was a class action suit that applied to all humanity. A class action suit is one in which the decision reached applies to all individuals in a particular group. The group may consist of everyone who has been affected by the use of a particular product. It may be a specific cultural class whose rights are being determined. The class Adam represented was every human being, born and yet to be born.
- Satan coming before the court of God to accuse Job and to obtain permission to test Job.
- Jesus appearing before God's throne with His own blood to pay for the sins of humanity and buy humanity back from the devil. Eternal life was awarded to the parties purchased

under this contract. This too was a class action suit. The class of people is all individuals who believe in the blood of Jesus Christ as being payment for their sins and who have received Jesus as their Savior.

- Eternal defeat and judgment were pronounced against Satan. His place will be in the lake of fire.
- The great throne judgment when people who have not been redeemed under the blood of Jesus will be judged and punished forever.

This is indeed a very brief summary of some of the legal aspects of God's justice. It would take a very long book to go into greater detail, which is not my intent. Instead, we will move ahead to the great redemption plan God brought us in Jesus.

Chapter 11
A Savior Comes

The last time we saw the Israelites, they had left Egypt and were traveling back to Canaan. God established them as a nation and brought them into the land where they would dwell as a people for God's purpose. His purpose was to establish a people and a lineage from which a Redeemer would come. This Redeemer would save people from every tribe and nation in the world. God would have the sons He intended from the foundation of the world.

The Israelites moved into the Promised Land of Israel. They conquered the various tribes and kingdoms that lived in the land until they controlled the whole area. They have a rich history of successes and failures, times when they ruled, and times when their enemies conquered them. God gave them rulers and leaders. Some were judges; others were kings. God sent them prophets to tell them what the future held and to foretell of the coming Redeemer. As the centuries rolled away, the time drew near for the Redeemer to be born into the world. Isaiah the prophet gives this prediction of the birth of Jesus in Isaiah 9:6–7:

> *For a child will be born to us, a son will be given to*
> *us; and the government will rest on His shoulders; and*
> *His name will be called Wonderful Counselor, Mighty*

*God, Eternal Father, Prince of Peace. There will be no
end to the increase of His government or of peace, on the
throne of David and over his kingdom, to establish it
and to uphold it with justice and righteousness from then
on and forevermore. The zeal of the Lord of hosts will
accomplish this.*

Nearly everyone is familiar with the birth of Jesus. We celebrate
this event every year at Christmas. Jesus was born to a virgin named
Mary and her engaged husband, Joseph, before they had sexual
relationships. Joseph waited until after Jesus was born to consummate
the marriage:

> *The birth of Jesus Christ came about this way: After His
> mother Mary had been engaged to Joseph, it was discovered
> before they came together that she was pregnant by the Holy
> Spirit. So her husband Joseph, being a righteous man, and
> not wanting to disgrace her publicly, decided to divorce her
> secretly. But after he had considered these things, an angel
> of the Lord suddenly appeared to him in a dream, saying,
> "Joseph, son of David, don't be afraid to take Mary as your
> wife, because what has been conceived in her is by the Holy
> Spirit. She will give birth to a son, and you are to name
> Him Jesus, because He will save His people from their
> sins." Now all this took place to fulfill what was spoken by
> the Lord through the prophet: See, the virgin will become
> pregnant and give birth to a son, and they will name Him
> Immanuel, which is translated "God is with us." When
> Joseph got up from sleeping, he did as the Lord's angel had
> commanded him. He married her but did not know her
> intimately until she gave birth to a son. And he named
> Him Jesus.*
>
> —Matt. 1:18–25 HCSB

Jesus was a special conception. The Holy Spirit of God over-shadowed Mary and fathered Jesus in Mary's womb. In Luke 1:35, an angel came to Mary with this message: "The angel answered and said to her [Mary], 'The Holy Spirit will come upon you, and the power of the Most High will overshadow you; and for that reason the holy offspring shall be called the Son of God.'" This creative act of God produced a Son who was literally God's offspring, with God's DNA, no impurity, no sin, and with untainted blood. God prepared a holy body for Jesus to inhabit. Hebrews 10:5 reads, "Therefore, when He comes into the world, He says, 'SACRIFICE AND OFFERING YOU HAVE NOT DESIRED, BUT A BODY YOU HAVE PREPARED FOR ME.'"

Animal blood and sacrifice down through the centuries had not been able to take away man's sin. Animal blood was of a different type than man's blood. It did not satisfy the legal requirement to pay for sin. We learn in Leviticus 17:11 that "it is the blood by reason of the life that makes atonement." Animal blood being innocent could cover sin, but it could not bring forgiveness for sin. Animal blood does not have eternal qualities and is not capable of carrying the life of the Holy Spirit, needed to restore life to man. The Redeemer had to be different. If the Redeemer's blood were sinful, it could never be a payment for sin, nor could it live eternally. If the Redeemer's blood were not capable of carrying the Holy Spirit, the Redeemer's blood could never restore life to man. Yes, Jesus's blood and body were different. If Jesus had been born in the normal human way, he would have carried the sin passed down by his parents. Since Jesus was created by divine act of His Father, God, Jesus's blood was like Adam's before he sinned, full of the Spirit and life. In fact, Jesus is called the last Adam in 1 Corinthians 15:45: "So also it is written, 'The first MAN, Adam, BECAME A LIVING SOUL.' The last Adam *became* a life-giving spirit."

Jesus developed as a child and grew into a man. He was unique among men, having a natural makeup like other people, but also having the spiritual side that other people did not have. He was fully man and fully God—Immanuel—God with us. He came to bring us back to what God meant us to be before Adam sinned. Jesus encountered the same temptations we encounter, and always had the choice to obey or disobey. We owe such immeasurable gratitude to Him that He always chose to obey His Father at all costs.

As Jesus approached thirty years of age, the time for His ministry to mankind was at hand. God had sent an ambassador named John the Baptist before Jesus to announce Jesus's ministry and prepare the people to receive Jesus's message. John was a relative of Jesus in the natural realm, with Jesus's mother Mary and John's mother thought to be cousins. John was proclaiming the news that the Kingdom of God was at hand and that people should repent from their sins in preparation for this event. The Jewish people had been looking for the Redeemer for centuries, and finally, the time had come. John was baptizing people in the Jordan River as they repented of their sins.

One day, Jesus came to the river and wanted to be baptized by John. John recognized that Jesus lived a sinless life and had no need to be baptized. But Jesus said He wanted to do everything right, so John consented to the baptism. When Jesus was baptized, the heavens opened and the Holy Spirit, in the manifested form of a dove, descended and stayed on Jesus. God had told John the Baptist that He would point out the Redeemer (Messiah) to him by this sign.

The Gospel of John tells us what John the Baptist had to say about Jesus:

> The next day John saw Jesus coming toward him and said, "Here is the Lamb of God, who takes away the sin of the world! This is the One I told you about: 'After me comes a man who has surpassed me, because He existed before me.' I didn't know Him, but I came baptizing with water so He might be revealed to Israel." And John testified, "I watched the Spirit descending from heaven like a dove,

and He rested on Him. I didn't know Him, but He who
sent me to baptize with water told me, 'The One you see
the Spirit descending and resting on—He is the One who
baptizes with the Holy Spirit.' I have seen and testified
that He is the Son of God!"

—John 1:29–34 HCSB

God the Father also audibly confirmed Jesus to be the promised Redeemer in Matthew 3:16–17: "After Jesus was baptized . . . there came a voice from heaven: This is My beloved Son. I take delight in Him" (HCSB)!

Yes, John the Baptist knew that Jesus was the long-awaited, appointed Savior. Animal sacrifice was coming to an end. Jesus was taking the place of the Lamb. He would become an effective sacrifice that would do more than just cover sin. His blood would pay for sin and take it away forever. The Spirit was upon Him. He was able to bear the Spirit's life, and that life would be restored to man. This would be a new covenant between God and man, cut in the blood of Jesus.

After Jesus's baptism, the Holy Spirit led Jesus into the wilderness to be tempted by the devil. The devil doesn't miss a beat in coming against God's plan. But Jesus fasted and fellowshipped with the Holy Spirit over a period of forty days. He grew strong in His purpose through communion with the Spirit. Then the devil tempted Jesus to serve his interests instead of God's. He hoped to trick Jesus by challenging God's Word like he had done with the first Adam and his companion, Eve. Praise God, the devil lost that battle! Jesus overcame the enemy by speaking the truth of God's Word. No rebellion from this Son! Jesus knew Who He was—the Word of God, sent forth in flesh from heaven to complete the work He came to do for mankind: to destroy the works of the devil! In 1 John 3:8, we are told that "the one who practices sin is of the devil; for the devil has sinned from the beginning. The Son of God appeared for this purpose, to destroy the works of the devil."

Works of the Devil

Since Jesus came specifically to destroy the works of the devil, we need to know exactly what that means. The first and foremost work the devil did was rob mankind of their position as sons of God. The rest of his evil work stems from that first work. We said earlier that Adam was a being with a natural physical side and a spiritual side. God breathed His Spirit into Adam when He created him. Because Adam received God's spiritual makeup, he was a son of God. Romans 8:14 says, "For all who are being led by the Spirit of God, these are sons of God."

In the beginning, Adam, Eve (who was made from Adam), and all their future children were considered sons of God. God's intent was that they would allow the Holy Spirit to lead and rule their lives. As long as they lived with the Spirit in charge, they had the awesome privilege of being sons of God and had dominion over all the natural realm. They owned the earth, and all it contained was under their dominion—as long as they believed God and obeyed Him.

This is what Satan was after. He had been a highly honored son of God, but in his rebellion, he had lost his heavenly position. He wanted the same thing to happen to man. He wanted people to forfeit their relationship with God and the dominion He had given them. Satan knew that once man stopped believing God's Word and rebelled against Him, the Spirit of God would leave man, and he would become just a natural, physical being, dead to the Spirit of God and no longer a son.

When man obeyed Satan, Satan became his owner, and man and the natural realm came under Satan's control. Satan became the world's ruler, and he ran it the way he wanted. Yes, he wanted to be a "god" over God's things in any way he could. As the world's devilish ruler, he had the authority to introduce all kinds of evil— sickness, pain, death, poverty and lack, slavery, hate, accidents, crime, and a multitude of other maladies. We know that is exactly what happened.

Satan won the first round, but God's redemption plan would bring Satan's defeat. Jesus came to destroy the evil work of the devil. Jesus came to put the Spirit of God back into those who would believe in the redeeming blood of Jesus. Once again, they would be restored to sonship with dominion over the world to rule in righteousness.

Prior to His baptism, Jesus had not performed any miracles during His earthly life. He was sinless, but He did not walk in any supernatural power. Once the Holy Spirit came upon Him, all that changed. He used the time that He spent in the wilderness to build a relationship with the Holy Spirit. Jesus returned from the wilderness temptation in the power of the Spirit (Luke 4:14). He began to preach and teach the message of the Kingdom of God. He healed, performed miracles, raised the dead, and put the devil on notice that the devil's time was drawing to an end. Many people believed Jesus's message and became his disciples. They learned to follow in His footsteps and to defeat the devil in their own lives:

> *And He came to Nazareth, where He had been brought up; and as was His custom, He entered the synagogue on the Sabbath, and stood up to read. And the book of the prophet Isaiah was handed to Him. And He opened the book, and found the place where it was written, "THE SPIRIT OF THE LORD IS UPON ME, BECAUSE HE ANOINTED ME TO PREACH THE GOSPEL TO THE POOR. HE HAS SENT ME TO PROCLAIM RELEASE TO THE CAPTIVES AND RECOVERY OF SIGHT TO THE BLIND, TO SET FREE THOSE WHO ARE OPPRESSED, TO PROCLAIM THE FAVORABLE YEAR OF THE LORD." And He closed the book, and gave it back to the attendant and sat down; and the eyes of all in the synagogue were fixed on Him. And He began to say to them, "Today this Scripture has been fulfilled in your hearing."*
>
> —Luke 4:16–21

Jesus ministered on the earth for three years. No greater love has ever been seen on earth than what He showed. The time for man's redemption had come.

The Passover was at hand. The Jewish nation had celebrated this annual feast for hundreds of years. It was a remembrance established by God to remind them of the time He redeemed them from slavery to the Pharaoh in Egypt. It was a type and picture of the future redemption God would achieve for His people in delivering them from the slavery and ownership of the devil. The Passover lamb was central to the redemption. In Egypt, the blood of the slain lamb covered the sins of the Jewish people and saved them from natural death. God passed over their sins and destroyed their enemy. Jesus came to take on that role of the Passover lamb to save a people from eternal spiritual death.

God had set up the redemption plan from the foundation of the world, and the devil and the ruling authorities played right into His hands: "And all that dwell upon the earth shall worship him [the devil], whose names are not written in the book of life of the **Lamb slain from the foundation of the world**" (Revelation 13:8 KJV). (emphasis added)

> *For you know that you were redeemed from your empty way of life inherited from the fathers, not with perishable things, like silver or gold, but with the precious blood of Christ, like that of a lamb without defect or blemish.* **He was chosen before the foundation of the world** *but was revealed at the end of the times for you who through Him are believers in God, who raised Him from the dead and gave Him glory, so that your faith and hope are in God.* (emphasis added)
>
> —1 Pet. 1:18–21 HCSB

God had put into effect His plan to redeem man by His own Son's blood even before man showed up on planet Earth.

The Jewish rulers hated Jesus. They were jealous of His influence, His challenging of their laws, the wisdom of His words, and of the miraculous signs He did. They were concerned about losing their control and position with the people. The devil hated Jesus as well, realizing the threat Jesus was to him.

Our foe, the devil, stirred up the people against Jesus so that they demanded His death. Jesus was sentenced to death on a cross and became the Passover lamb. Not only did Jesus become the Passover lamb, but He also became the scapegoat that the Jews had offered every year on the Day of Atonement. Like the scapegoat of long ago, the totality of all mankind's sin was transferred to and laid on Jesus for Him to bear.

Like the Passover lamb, Jesus's blood was shed as a sacrifice for the sins of mankind. On the cross, blood poured over Jesus's whole body from multiple wounds, making a complete blood covering of all man's sin. However, the blood not only covered man's sin, it paid the death penalty for our sin. As stated in Romans 6:23, "the wages of sin is death." Jesus took our death penalty so that we would not have to.

As Jesus hung on the cross in our place, God the Father poured out his righteous wrath and judgment against our sin. There in the body of Jesus Christ, our sin was eternally judged and condemned. Our Savior bore it for us in our place.

Jesus carried our sins away into the wilderness of Hell where He left them. Sin no longer has a right to hold us. The devil, the one who had held the power of death, was spoiled and defeated. How do we know?

Because Jesus rose from the dead! The death penalty for sin could no longer hold Him or us. His holy blood won over sin! Colossians 2:15 says, "He [God] disarmed the rulers and authorities and disgraced them [demonic forces] publicly; He triumphed over them by Him" (HCSB).

On the third day after Jesus's crucifixion, Jesus bodily rose from the dead by the power of God's Spirit. His sacrifice for man's sin fulfilled the law's requirement of death for sinning and was accepted in heaven's courtroom as payment for our sins.

But on the first day of the week, at early dawn, they [the disciples] came to the tomb, bringing the spices which they had prepared. And they found the stone rolled away from the tomb, but when they entered, they did not find the body of the Lord Jesus. While they were perplexed about this, behold, two men suddenly stood near them in dazzling clothing; and as the women *were terrified and bowed their faces to the ground,* the men *said to them, "Why do you seek the living One among the dead? He is not here, but He has risen. Remember how He spoke to you while He was still in Galilee, saying that the Son of Man must be delivered into the hands of sinful men, and be crucified, and the third day rise again." And they remembered His words, and returned from the tomb and reported all these things to the eleven and to all the rest.*

—Luke 24:1–9

After Jesus's resurrection, He entered heaven's throne room itself with His own eternal blood, where it was accepted by Father God for our eternal redemption.

But when Christ appeared as a high priest of the good things to come, He entered *through the greater and more perfect tabernacle, not made with hands, that is to say, not of this creation; and not through the blood of goats and calves, but through His own blood, He entered the holy place once for all, having obtained eternal redemption. For if the blood of goats and bulls and the ashes of a heifer sprinkling those who have been defiled sanctify for the cleansing of the flesh, how much more will the blood of Christ, who through the eternal Spirit offered Himself without blemish to God, cleanse your conscience from dead works to serve the living God?*

—Heb. 9:11–14

For Christ did not enter a holy place made with hands, a mere copy of the true one, but into heaven itself, now to appear in the presence of God for us; nor was it that He should offer Himself often, as the high priest enters the holy place year by year with blood not his own. Otherwise, He would have needed to suffer often since the foundation of the world; but now once at the consummation of the ages He has been manifested to put away sin by the sacrifice of Himself. And inasmuch as it is appointed for men to die once and after this comes *judgment, so Christ also, having been offered once to bear the sins of many, will appear a second time for salvation without* reference to *sin, to those who eagerly await Him.*

—Heb. 9: 24–28

After Jesus rose from the dead and took His blood into the great throne room (courtroom) of heaven to pay for our redemption, He spent another forty days on the earth before taking up residence again in heaven, where He will remain until the end of the age. What did He do during those forty days prior to His departure? He did some very important things:

1. *Hope Restored and Forgiveness Experienced:* When Jesus was crucified, the disciples were devastated. They believed all was lost. Their hope was gone and their dreams smashed. They were overwhelmed with grief and in fear of the Jewish leaders. When Jesus rose, it changed everything. Jesus was alive! They saw Him! Grief turned to joy. Everything Jesus had told them was true. Death was conquered, and they had an eternal hope. He spent time with them eating, teaching, fishing, and speaking about things of the kingdom of God. Jesus especially reached out to Peter, who had denied Him three times during Jesus's trial. Peter received Jesus's forgiveness and reassurance of his acceptance.

2. *The Scriptures Explained:* Jesus spent time with the disciples explaining the scriptures that had predicted His coming and what He would achieve. He showed them how He had fulfilled every one of the predictions. At one point after His resurrection, Jesus walked with two disciples as they journeyed to the town of Emmaus. These disciples were perplexed and sad about the crucifixion and resurrection events. After Jesus rebuked them for their unbelief, He went on to explain the meaning of the Old Testament Scriptures.

And He said to them, "O foolish men and slow of heart to believe in all that the prophets have spoken! Was it not necessary for the Christ to suffer these things and to enter into His glory?" Then beginning with Moses and with all the prophets, He explained to them the things concerning Himself in all the Scriptures.

—Luke 24:25–27

Later the same day, Jesus appeared to the eleven apostles and to some others who were with them. He showed them His hands and feet that had been pierced and nailed to the cross. He ate with them to show them He was not just a dream. Then He helped them to understand the Scriptures that had been written about Him.

Now He said to them, "These are My words which I spoke to you while I was still with you, that all things which are written about Me in the Law of Moses and the Prophets and the Psalms must be fulfilled." Then He opened their minds to understand the Scriptures, and He said to them, "Thus it is written, that the Christ should suffer and rise again from the dead the third day; and that repentance for forgiveness of sins would be proclaimed in His name to all the nations, beginning from Jerusalem. You are witnesses of these things."

—Luke 24:44–48

3. *Sonship Restored by the Holy Spirit:* Jesus breathed the Holy Spirit back into the believing disciples, restoring them to the position of sons of God. They were no longer slaves of Satan. They were new creatures destined to rule and reign with Jesus, the Son of God.

So Jesus said to them again, "Peace be with you; as the Father has sent Me, I also send you." And when He had said this, He breathed on them, and said to them, "Receive the Holy Spirit."

—John 20:21–22

Therefore if anyone is in Christ, he is a new creature; the old things passed away; behold, new things have come.

—2 Cor. 5:17

4. *Baptism in the Holy Spirit—the Spirit's Empowerment:* Jesus gave the disciples instructions as to what they were to do after He departed for heaven. He commanded them that they were to stay in Jerusalem and wait for the promise that God the Father had made centuries earlier. This was a promise that God would pour out His Holy Spirit on mankind to empower them in their roles as sons of God. This empowerment would give them what they needed in their transition from natural man to spiritual man. They would become witnesses of what God had done and be able to live a life of victory over Satan.

To these He also presented Himself alive, after His suffering, by many convincing proofs, appearing to them over a period of forty days and speaking of the things concerning the kingdom of God. Gathering them together, He commanded them not to leave Jerusalem, but to wait for what the Father had promised, "Which," He said, "you heard of from Me; for John baptized with water, but you will be baptized with the Holy Spirit not many days from now." So when they had come together, they were asking Him, saying, "Lord, is it at this time You are restoring the kingdom to Israel?" He said to them, "It is not for you to know times or epochs which the Father has fixed by His own authority; but you will receive power when the Holy Spirit has come upon you; and you shall be My witnesses both in Jerusalem, and in all Judea and Samaria, and even to the remotest part of the earth."

—Acts 1:3–8

5. *The Great Commission:* Jesus gave them a job to do—tell the rest of the world about the redemption Christ achieved. This is commonly known as the "Great Commission."

    And Jesus came up and spoke to them, saying, "All authority has been given to Me in heaven and on earth. Go therefore and make disciples of all the nations, baptizing them in the name of the Father and the Son and the Holy Spirit, teaching them to observe all that I commanded you; and lo, I am with you always, even to the end of the age."

    —Matt. 28:18–20

The disciples went forth and did what Jesus told them to do. He promised to give them what they needed to get the job done and that He would always be with them.

So then, when the Lord Jesus had spoken to them, He was received up into heaven and sat down at the right hand of God. And they went out and preached everywhere, while the Lord worked with them, and confirmed the word by the signs that followed.

—Mark 16:19–20

Chapter 12
Definitions of Some Important Biblical Terms

A
s we get ready to examine God's righteousness and what He has made us in Christ, let's define some words in preparation for what we will discuss.

Apostle   One who is sent to bring the message of salvation through Jesus Christ to others to enable them to become obedient to faith in Him.

Atonement   A covering. A blanket that cannot be seen through.

Born Again   A natural man into whom the Spirit of God has been implanted and conceived and Who has brought forth a new spiritual man—a new creation. This is a new race of man, a son of God. The person is no longer like the old Adam. He is like the Last Adam, Jesus Christ—a spiritual man living in a natural body. He is to constantly put to death the fleshly nature and be led and controlled by the Spirit of God now living in him.

Christ/Messiah	The anointed one—the one who carries the Holy Spirit. The Holy Spirit has been "smeared on" Him and He bears the Spirit's presence.
Faith	Faith is the way to the hope/end. You make a firm decision to believe, trust, speak, and act toward that hope until it is manifested.
Gentile	Everyone who is not a Jew.
Glorified	Changed into the image of Christ so that we manifest and reveal the character and acts of God to those around us. While we are in the body, it is a process from glory to glory. We will be totally glorified, our glorification complete, at the second coming of Jesus when our body is exchanged for a spiritual body when the sons of God are revealed.
Glory	The revelation/manifestation of God's goodness as seen in His character and acts.
Gospel	The good news message we preach to everyone that because of the blood of Jesus, God now deals in grace to those who believe the message.
Grace	The exact opposite of wrath. It is given by God as a gift that has been purchased by the blood of Jesus Christ. It is everything we need for life and godliness. It includes all of God's goodness smiling on us.
Hope	The assured result, the expected end. Hope is the full assurance of the achievement of the good expected end.

Justified	Being justified clears us of sin. Sin is wiped from our account because of the resurrection of Jesus.
Propitiation	One who steps in as a substitute to take the deserved wrath from a wronged party that is being poured out on the perpetrator. Not only did Jesus receive all God's wrath meant for us, but after the wrath was spent, He turned God's wrath into love, grace, and goodness toward us. A scapegoat.
Repent	To change your way of thinking about something; to correct it from wrong or unholy thinking to right or holy thinking and allow the change in thinking to transform your corresponding behavior.
Righteousness	Means being right with God and includes acting in ways that God sees as right. God declares us right. We cannot earn it. It is by faith. Belief in the blood of Jesus to pay for our sins enables God to credit righteousness to us.
Saint	One who is born again and making the trip from the earthly image to the spiritual image of Christ.
Sanctified	Set aside as saints to be changed from natural beings into spiritual beings. We are new creatures from the time of salvation, born again as soon as the Spirit of God enters our hearts. It is a lifelong process of putting to death the fleshly nature and being conformed to the spiritual man we will put on fully upon entering heaven.

Son of God   One who is led by the Spirit of God and has God's spiritual makeup. The term applies to both males and females without distinction. It is a title that reflects position, adoption, authority, and inheritance rather than gender and sex. Under Jewish law, typically the father's inheritance would go only to sons, and authority was held by males. In Christ, both males and females are equally considered sons.

As another example, the church is called the Bride of Christ and it is composed of both males and females. It is a reflection of position and role rather than gender. Scripture further supports emphasis on the position of the believer rather than on the believer's gender/roots in Galatians 3:28: "There is neither Jew nor Greek, there is neither slave nor free man, there is neither male nor female; for you are all one in Christ Jesus."

Chapter 13

God's Righteousness Apart from the Law

We began this book by talking about the righteousness of God. God has always been righteous, but before Christ, the only way He could righteously deal with sin was through the law, which brought wrath and judgment. Now we are going to talk about God's righteous dealing with us apart from the law. Some of the most liberating and hopeful verses we can ever read are found in Romans:

> But now, apart from the law, God's righteousness has been revealed—attested by the Law and the Prophets—that is, God's righteousness through faith in Jesus Christ, to all who believe, since there is no distinction. For all have sinned and fall short of the glory of God. They are justified freely by His grace through the redemption that is in Christ Jesus. God presented Him as a

propitiation through faith in His blood, to demonstrate
His righteousness, because in His restraint God passed
over the sins previously committed. God presented Him
to demonstrate His righteousness at the present time, so
that He would be righteous and declare righteous the one
who has faith in Jesus.

—Rom. 3:21–26 HCSB

Now I want to put these verses in words that will make them clear and simple to understand and provide the impact they should give in our lives. Holy Spirit, help me to paraphrase these verses under your anointing:

God's character of always acting right has been shown in a way that is totally different from the way He dealt with people according to what He was bound to do by the law. Under the law, God was always legally required to bring judgment and wrath for sin. But the law and the prophets both foretold of a time when God would still act righteously when He laid aside the wrath and dealt in grace with sinners. God would legally be counted righteous in dealing with people this way when they had faith in Jesus Christ. There would be no distinction in treatment between Jew and Gentile, good and bad. The provision is for everyone who believes. By the law, everyone has sinned and fallen short of the glory—the expected, God-like behavior God requires. So God, by His grace, has freely cleared those who believe in the redemption found in Jesus Christ.

God presented Jesus as the One who took the deserved wrath of God against mankind. He was the scapegoat. He stood in man's place and bore the anger and punishment of God for us, until it was spent and God's anger was turned to kindness toward us. The wrath turns to kindness when we put our trust in the blood Jesus shed for our sins. The blood turns God's grace into righteous behavior and clears God from any perceived unrighteousness He may have been accused of when He restrained from wrathful judgment for previously committed sins. God presented Jesus and what Jesus did to show everyone right now that God is righteous always, with the law or without it, and so that God could declare righteous (right with God) the one who has faith in Jesus.

—Romans 3:21–26 (Paraphrased)

Devil, you lose. God dealt with you rightly. God has dealt with man rightly. Thank you, Father, that you provided the way in Jesus to be merciful, forgiving, and full of grace to us. "Amazing love! How can it be, That Thou, my God, shouldst die for me?"[4]

---

4. Charles Wesley, "And Can It Be?" hymn, 1738.

Chapter 14

The Blood of the Eternal Covenant

The Old Covenant was administered by the Levitical priesthood. Aaron, the first high priest, was a descendant from the Jewish tribe of Levi. Levi was the third son of Jacob and his wife, Leah. All priests were taken from the tribe of Levi, and no one could be appointed to the office unless he was from that tribe. According to Numbers 17, God chose from among the Levites the household of Aaron from which high priests would descend. When the high priest died, a new one would take over in his place.

The Israelites received the Law from God, and it was the work of the Levitical priesthood to administer it. And it was work indeed—always laboring to be good enough by the Law's standard. The Law is perfect, but people are not, and the Law cannot make anyone perfect. It was and is ineffective in changing hearts. It was time for a change—time for a new priesthood with a change in the Law.

The New Covenant brought a change in the priesthood and how it is administered. The new priesthood is in complete contrast to the Levitical priesthood. God made the promise under oath that He would institute this new priesthood, saying in Hebrews 7:11: "If, then, perfection came through the Levitical priesthood (for under it the people received the law), what further need was there for another priest to appear, said to be in the order of Melchizedek and not in the order of Aaron?" (HCSB)

God instituted the new priesthood with a high priest who resembled Melchizedek who served God as a priest during Abraham's days, centuries before Levi was born. Melchizedek may have been a pre-incarnation of Jesus; he was known as King of Salem and priest of the Most High God. His name meant "king of righteousness" and "king of peace." His life had no beginning or end and was likened to the Son of God.

God ordained Jesus to be the One who would administer this new, unending, and better priesthood. God went on to make a promise to Jesus, saying, "The Lord has sworn, and He will not change His mind, You are a priest forever" (Hebrews 7:21 HCSB). After His resurrection, Jesus took His sacrificial blood to the throne room of heaven and became our High Priest forever. He lives eternally to represent believers before God and give them grace on the basis of faith in His blood rather than on their efforts to keep the Law.

Jesus was not from the tribe of Levi, but rather from the tribe of Judah, from which no one had ever served as a priest. He is known as the Lion of the tribe of Judah. We can only speculate as to why God appointed the tribe of Judah from which our eternal Priest would come. But I would like to give a possible explanation for consideration, and you may do with it what you choose.

As we look back on Jewish history, we are reminded that Jacob was the patriarchal father of twelve sons who grew into the twelve tribes of Israel. However, there is more to the story. Jacob had two wives and two concubines (slaves of his two wives who also bore him children). The mothers of the twelve sons played an important part in what happened.

Jacob was a rather tricky fellow before he met God. Jacob, with his mother's help, tricked his brother Esau out of the birthright and blessing that belonged to Esau. Because of the trickery, Esau was cheated out of his inheritance and authority as a firstborn son. Jacob fled to his uncle's land to escape the wrath of his brother.

While Jacob took up residence at his uncle's homestead, Jacob fell in love with his uncle's daughter, Rachel. He made a deal with his uncle, Laban, to work for him for seven years in exchange for Rachel's hand in marriage. But Laban was quite the trickster himself. After the seven years, it was time for the marriage. Laban held a feast for the local men, which culminated in the wedding night. This was the time well before electric lights. Laban brought the bride to the wedding chamber. When daylight came, Jacob found that Laban had brought his oldest daughter, Leah, to Jacob instead of Rachel. Laban told Jacob that it was not their custom to marry off the younger before the older daughter. Talk about a disappointment! However, intent upon his purpose, Jacob agreed to work another seven years to get Rachel, the woman he really loved.

Once Jacob and Rachel were married, you can imagine the friction in the household with a couple of wives and the two slaves that came with them. Leah was clearly unwanted and scorned. God saw that Leah was unloved, so He blessed her by giving her children. However, Rachel remained barren for a long time before having two sons. Every time Leah had a son, she hoped that it would win the love and favor of her husband, Jacob. She said, "The LORD has seen my affliction; surely my husband will love me now" (Genesis 29:32b HCSB). Three times she bore sons, but it did not change anything.

Then Leah had a change of heart. The fourth son came, and Leah made the decision to trust God, give thanks, and refuse to grumble or be disappointed over her circumstances. "And she conceived again, gave birth to a son, and said, 'This time I will praise the LORD.' Therefore she named him Judah" (Genesis 29:35 HCSB).

Leah could not change her circumstances, but she could change her attitude and trust God. God took her trust in Him and her praise and turned her situation into a memorial to her forever. Even though she had been the mother of the tribe of Levi, she became the mother of the tribe of Judah from which our Lord came—the Lion of the tribe of Judah. The Lion who turned our situation around—bold, overcoming and defeating our enemy forever.

Let's go back to comparing the two priesthoods. Hebrews 7:28 tells us that "the law appoints as high priests men who are weak, but the promise of the oath, which came after the law, appoints a Son, who has been perfected forever" (HCSB).

Under the law, Levitical priests were limited by their own sinfulness and offerings that could not permanently wipe out sin. Under the promises of the New Covenant, which set up the priesthood of Jesus, the one offering that Jesus made of His own life and blood permanently paid for and cleansed the sin of people. Jesus stands as the perfect Son of God able to save and perfect man forever.

The purpose of a priest is to represent sinners before God. Hebrews 5:1 says, "For every high priest taken from men is appointed in service to God for the people, to offer both gifts and sacrifices for sins" (HCSB).

Throughout this book, we have proclaimed the infinite value of blood. Millions of animals were slain during the history of the world and under the Levitical priesthood. The value of those animals and their blood cannot be measured. But all that blood did not wipe out our sin. It only reminded us of our shortcomings. The blood was offered daily to cover both the priests' sins and the people's sins. It was not a permanent fix and could not restore our relationship with God.

Jesus's priesthood is different. His sacrificial gift of Himself, offered one time, restored our relationship with God. His blood is special and powerful. Although we know not the means, after Jesus was raised from the dead, His blood, full of the Spirit of God, is the one physical substance that Jesus transported from earth to the heavenly throne room of the Father and sprinkled on God's throne. It is the one physical substance we know to exist in heaven. It was accepted by the Father for man's eternal redemption.

Jesus's blood is eternal and perpetual. It never dies. Its power never stops. There is no interruption or intermission in its effectiveness. The blood of Jesus and the Spirit speak for us legally and plead our case before the throne of God. At all times, we can come boldly to our Father's throne on the grounds of the shed blood of Jesus in faith that what God has promised in His word has been obtained and given to us through the blood of Jesus. Our Father's arms are open wide to us.

The blood avails for us here and now in the natural and spiritual realms and throughout eternity. It will take our souls that have been declared righteous through faith in the blood and make them perfect for eternity. It is the keeping and staying ability of the powerful blood of Jesus that will keep us from falling forever.

Chapter 15

Who We Are in Christ

The position we have in Christ is truly amazing and beyond the realm of what most of us realize. All we have comes through the faith we have in Jesus's blood. Through the blood of Jesus, we are brought into a blessed relationship with God. That is huge! Let's examine the riches Jesus obtained for us.

Declared Righteous by God

The first benefit God gives us when we believe in Jesus is a change in what God has to say about us. He no longer calls us children of wrath, sinners, and disobedient. Instead he declares us to be righteous or, more simply put, right with Him. Faith in the blood of Jesus brings us into right standing with God.

Prior to the shed blood of Jesus, God had to deal with everyone through the Law (of Sin and Death). There was little room for grace and mercy. You had to keep the whole Law or be punished—the punishment being death. But now, Jesus has fulfilled the requirement of the Law on both counts—keeping it and being punished by it. First, Jesus lived a sinless life. He never broke the Law. He was righteous and always in right standing with His Father. He was never under judgment for His own sins. Second, He fulfilled the Law's requirement of punishment for breaking the Law—not punishment for Himself, but rather punishment for us instead. He was punished in our place for our sins. He bore our penalty. His death became our death. It was an acceptable substitution.

The court of heaven declared that the Law was satisfied and that justice had been met by Jesus's holy blood that had been shed as payment for mankind's sin. Jesus was cleared of all guilt and raised from the dead. Since the Holy Spirit joins us to Jesus, we share in the same standing and benefits Jesus has. Jesus is righteous, and we are declared righteous with Him. We share Jesus's righteousness. This is a gift from God. It is a new system in heaven that God is operating under called grace. It is the opposite of judgment and wrath. This is favor apart from the Law. Second Corinthians 5:21 tells us, "He made Him who knew no sin *to be* sin on our behalf, that we might become the righteousness of God in Him."

Jesus's blood cleansed us from all sin. When God looks at us now, He no longer sees our sin, but rather the blood covering of Jesus's precious blood on our lives. We need to honor that blood and thank God for it daily. First John 1:7 assures us that "the blood of Jesus His Son **cleanses us from all sin**." (emphasis added)

Justified

Not only are we declared righteous because of our faith, we are justified. That means we have been cleared of all charges and condemnation against us. Righteousness and justification go hand in hand. When God declares us right, we are no longer under judgment. So often, the devil will whisper in our ear that we are unworthy, stupid, and hopeless. He causes us to doubt that we have been cleared by the King. The devil is a liar. God sees us as forgiven children that He has adopted and brought into His household.

Now to the one who works, his wage is not credited as a favor, but as what is due. But to the one who does not work, but believes in Him who **justifies** *the ungodly, his* **faith** *is credited as righteousness, just as David also speaks of the blessing on the man to whom God credits righteousness apart from works: "BLESSED ARE THOSE WHOSE LAWLESS DEEDS HAVE BEEN FORGIVEN, AND WHOSE SINS HAVE BEEN COVERED. BLESSED IS THE MAN WHOSE SIN THE LORD WILL NOT TAKE INTO ACCOUNT."* (emphasis added)

—Rom. 4:4–8

All the decrees and judgments against us have been canceled. Colossians 2:13-14 says:

He [God] made you alive together with Him [Jesus], having forgiven us all our transgressions, having canceled out the certificate of debt consisting of decrees against us, which was hostile to us; and He has taken it out of the way, having nailed it to the cross.

Abraham, the father of faith and of many nations, had been declared righteous with God long before Jesus came to earth due to his faith and obedience to use the blood covering God provided in animals. However, Abraham's account was not cleared until the cross. It took the blood of Jesus to clear and justify people with God. Once that holy blood had been shed and Jesus rose from the dead, all the righteous faithful down through the generations were together cleared and justified with God!

Peace with God—the Curse of the Law Removed

Because of being declared righteous and justified, we now have peace with God—no wrath, no anger, no judgment, no condemnation! We no longer are under the Curse of the Law. In a previous chapter, we talked about the time in the wilderness when the Israelites were given the Law. With the Law came curses for failure to keep the Law. But Jesus became a curse for us and set us free from punishment and brought us into the blessings of God!

> For as many as are of the works of the Law are under a curse; for it is written, "CURSED IS EVERYONE WHO DOES NOT ABIDE BY ALL THINGS WRITTEN IN THE BOOK OF THE LAW, TO PERFORM THEM." Christ redeemed us from the curse of the Law, having become a curse for us—for it is written, "CURSED IS EVERYONE WHO HANGS ON A TREE"—in order that in Christ Jesus the blessing of Abraham might come to the Gentiles, so that we would receive the promise of the Spirit through faith.
>
> —Gal. 3:10, 13–14

In place of the curses, we now have all the blessings the Holy Spirit brings into our lives. The Holy Spirit works all things together for our good for us who love God and are called according to the great purpose He had in redeeming us.

A Sure Hope

God has given us a sure hope to exult in. We can be sure that we will experience eternal life, the glory of God, and all that heaven and sonship have to offer. Romans 5:2 says, "We have also obtained access through Him by faith into this grace in which we stand, and we rejoice in the hope of the glory of God" (HCSB).

Eternal Life

We have previously quoted part of Romans 6:23 that tells of the wages of sin being death. But Christ has turned that verse around, and we can now read the rest of the verse: "But the free gift of God is eternal life in Christ Jesus our Lord."

Sanctified

Man, in his sinful state, was formerly expendable. But now the blood of Christ has assigned us great worth. God saves the believer and sets him apart (sanctifies him) for a holy use. God does this special work in all he calls to be His sons. God has a special plan for each person, unique to that individual. The Holy Spirit equips and leads each son in the way he is to go, so it is very important to develop a close communion with the Spirit and follow His leading. A sanctified one is called a saint, so all those who are believers in the blood of Jesus Christ for their salvation are called saints.

Crucified with Christ—Raised to Walk in Newness of Life

Romans 6 tells us that we have been baptized into the death of Jesus. We are identified with Him in a class action suit. What applies to Him, applies to all believers. His death becomes our death. Likewise, we are united with Him in His resurrection. We die to sin and are raised to walk in newness of life through the indwelling Holy Spirit deposited in us. As we become more and more familiar with the Holy Spirit's voice and character, we will walk more and more like Jesus did.

> *Or do you not know that all of us who have been baptized into Christ Jesus have been baptized into His death? Therefore we have been buried with Him through baptism into death, so that as Christ was raised from the dead through the glory of the Father, so we too might walk in newness of life.*
>
> —Rom. 6:3–4

Filled with and Led by the Holy Spirit

When Adam and Eve sinned, the most devastating consequence they experienced was the departure of the Holy Spirit from their physical bodies. The results were all-encompassing. Through the Holy Spirit, they had experienced the presence of God. With the Holy Spirit gone, they no longer had fellowship and intimacy with God. They no longer could walk in the cool of the Garden of Eden with Him. The Life of the Holy Spirit was no longer in them to sustain their bodies. They lost dominion of the earth and forfeited control to the devil. They were no longer considered sons of God. They were just natural beings without a future or hope.

The blood of Jesus Christ changed all this. Restoring the Holy Spirit back into mankind and the resulting rebirth of the sons of God was the Promise and became the focal point down through the centuries for both God and man. Because of Abraham's faith, God honored him by making Abraham the father of faith and of nations. God promised Abraham that He would put the Spirit back into people through their faith in Jesus Christ. Once again, we will quote that promise from Galatians 3:13–14:

> *Christ redeemed us from the curse of the Law, having become a curse for us—for it is written, "Cursed is everyone who hangs on a tree"—in order that in Christ Jesus the blessing of Abraham might come to the Gentiles,* **so that we would receive the promise of the Spirit through faith.** (emphasis added)

The blood of Jesus received by faith puts the Holy Spirit back into a person, makes the individual into a son of God, adopted into God's family and made a new creation. Praise God for redeeming and restoring!

Sealed by the Holy Spirit

The Holy Spirit is God's stamp of ownership on us. He is the down payment for God to take possession of us. He is the start of our conversion from a natural state into a fully spiritual state when we leave this body and take up residence in our new spiritual body.

We have also received an inheritance in Him [Jesus], predestined according to the purpose of the One who works out everything in agreement with the decision of His will. . . . When you heard the message of truth, the gospel of your salvation—and when you believed in Him, you were also sealed with the promised Holy Spirit. He [Holy Spirit] is the down payment of our inheritance, for the redemption of the possession, to the praise of His glory.

—Eph. 1:11, 13–14 HCSB

Glorified

By the Holy Spirit, we are made into beings who manifest the nature of God. As we submit to the leading of the Holy Spirit and follow His instructions, the Spirit of God can operate through us to act in the character and power of God. The good and loving character of God is revealed through us.

This hope will not disappoint us, because God's love has been poured out in our hearts through the Holy Spirit who was given to us.

—Rom. 5:5 HCSB

For those He foreknew He also predestined to be conformed to the image of His Son, so that He would be the firstborn among many brothers. And those He predestined, He also called; and those He called, He also justified; and those He justified, He also glorified.

—Rom. 8:29–30 HCSB

Yes, God's plan before man was ever created was to redeem a people to be like His Son, Jesus Christ. His redemption plan involved calling out people to be cleared of all wrong so that they could be living proof of the nature, power, and goodness of God—sons like their Father and big Brother.

Rule and Reign in Life

Through Jesus and what He obtained in the class action suit, we have acquired so much. The original case against the first Adam brought death to all. Jesus reversed that first case against us. Death reigned through the sin of Adam. Life and righteousness reign through the obedience of Jesus Christ, and we partake of that reality in Christ.

Romans 5:17 says, "Since by the one man's trespass, death reigned through that one man, how much more will those who receive the overflow of grace and the gift of righteousness reign in life through the one man, Jesus Christ" (HCSB).

Joint Heirs with Christ

We inherit all the things that Jesus inherits from the Father. He shares it all with us.

> *The Spirit Himself testifies together with our spirit that we are God's children, and if children, also heirs—heirs of God and coheirs with Christ—seeing that we suffer with Him so that we may also be glorified with Him.*
>
> —Rom. 8:16–17 HCSB

> *He predestined us to be adopted through Jesus Christ for Himself, according to His favor and will.*
>
> —Eph. 1:5 HCSB

God gives us everything we need for life and godliness. He gives us wonderful promises and allows us to share His own nature.

> *His divine power has given us everything required for life and godliness, through the knowledge of Him who called us by His own glory and goodness. By these He has given us very great and precious promises, so that through them you may share in the divine nature.*
>
> —2 Pet. 1:3–4 HCSB

Part of the Body of Christ—the Church

Jesus received a glorified body when He was raised from the dead. This body will never again die. He can appear through walls without going through doors. He can be in one place one minute and another place the next minute. He is not bound by gravity but rose up into heaven on a cloud when He went back to heaven. We don't know what it all involves now, but we are told that when He returns to receive us back to Himself at the end of the age, we will be like Him because we will see Him as He is.

When Jesus left the earth and returned to heaven, we are told that He sat down at the right hand of God to rule and reign in a position of authority. The Bible uses the picture of a natural body to explain spiritual truth, saying the church is comparable to a physical body. Jesus Himself as the head is in the position of authority over the body, and He has made each believer a part of His body. In each body, there must be unity among the members for the body to work properly. Similarly, each of us has a special place and function in His body, but no one part is more important or needed than another. Someone may function as a hand or foot, while another may fill the role of a mouth or ear. Each part (person) is essential to the functioning of the whole, and working together, we become the means through which God ministers throughout the earth today. We are honored to co-labor with the Lord under the direction of His Holy Spirit. And as in times of old, the Holy Spirit will confirm God's truth that we speak and do with signs and wonders that follow us. God has put us in a position seated with Jesus in heavenly spiritual places so that we may make Him known in the earth today. As the world sees His body, the church, acting in the power and love of God, people are drawn to know Him in His true character of goodness and love.

Ponder the claims made in the following verses:

He [God] demonstrated this power in the Messiah by raising Him from the dead and seating Him at His right hand in the heavens—far above every ruler and authority, power and dominion, and every title given, not only in this age but also in the one to come. And **He put everything under His feet** *and appointed Him as head over everything for the church, which is His body, the fullness of the One who fills all things in every way.* (emphasis added)

—Eph. 1:20–23 HCSB

But God, who is rich in mercy, because of His great love that He had for us, made us alive with the Messiah even though we were dead in trespasses. You are saved by grace! Together with Christ Jesus **He also raised us up and seated us in the heavens, so that in the coming ages He might display the immeasurable riches of His grace in His kindness to us in Christ Jesus.** *For you are saved by grace through faith, and this is not from yourselves; it is God's gift—not from works, so that no one can boast. For we are His creation, created in Christ Jesus for good works, which God prepared ahead of time so that we should walk in them.* (emphasis added)

—Eph. 2:4–10 HCSB

Authority

Please especially pay attention to the truth that we are raised up and seated with Jesus in the heavens. He shares His authority with us, and we rule and reign with Him in life over all evil we encounter. Satan is defeated. We have overcome him by the blood of the Lamb and the word of our testimony (what we say). Don't let the enemy run your life!

Jesus has given us authority. Let's use it and do the work He has given us.

When the crowds saw this, they were awestruck and gave glory to God who had given such authority to men.

—Matt. 9:8 HCSB

Look, I have given you the authority to trample on snakes and scorpions and over all the power of the enemy; nothing will ever harm you.

—Luke 10:19 HCSB

And Jesus came up and spoke to them, saying, "All authority has been given to Me in heaven and on earth. Go therefore and make disciples of all the nations, baptizing them in the name of the Father and the Son and the Holy Spirit, teaching them to observe all that I commanded you; and lo, I am with you always, even to the end of the age."

—Matt. 28:18–20

Other Things We Are in Christ

There are so many things we have in Christ that it is hard to cover it all. I have tried to cover some of the major topics. I will list a few more without going into detail. You may use a good concordance and continue to study them.

- We have the mind of Christ (1 Corinthians 2:16).
- We are ambassadors of Christ (2 Corinthians 5:20).
- We are the fragrance of Christ to God (2 Corinthians 2:15).
- We are witnesses of Christ (Acts 1:8).
- We are "A CHOSEN RACE, A royal PRIESTHOOD, A HOLY NATION, A PEOPLE FOR *God's* OWN POSSESSION" (1 Peter 2:9).

Chapter 16

The Holy Spirit—Help along the Way

I will ask the Father, and He will give you another Helper,
that He may be with you forever; that is the Spirit of truth,
whom the world cannot receive, because it does not see Him or
know Him, but you know Him because He abides with you
and will be in you.

—John 14:16–17

The Holy Spirit is the gift God promised Abraham that He would give to those who believe in Jesus. He is truly our helper. When Jesus came, He promised that He would ask the Father to send the Helper, as John 14:16–17 explains.

When Jesus was ministering on the earth, He told His disciples they should ask for good gifts and the Father would give them their requests. Jesus explains:

> *So I say to you, ask, and it will be given to you; seek, and*
> *you will find; knock, and it will be opened to you. For*
> *everyone who asks, receives; and he who seeks, finds; and*

to him who knocks, it will be opened. Now suppose one of
you fathers is asked by his son for a fish; he will not give him
a snake instead of a fish, will he? Or if he is asked for an
egg, he will not give him a scorpion, will he? If you then,
being evil, know how to give good gifts to your children,
how much more will your *heavenly Father give the Holy*
Spirit to those who ask Him?

—Luke 11:9–13

The Holy Spirit is present throughout our entire life journey from start to finish, guiding us and teaching us to be like Jesus. He is part of the Godhead along with Father God and Jesus Christ. He lives within us in intimate fellowship so that we can know God, and He helps us understand the Word of God and learn how to apply its truths to our lives.

God tells us that if we lack wisdom, we should ask Him and He will gladly give it to us. How does God impart this wisdom? The Spirit is the One who brings revelation to our hearts. As you read scripture, meditate on it, and ask the Holy Spirit to give you understanding. When you mull over passages again and again and meditate on what you read, the Spirit will show you truth and teach you meaning. We will enumerate the many ways the Holy Spirit helps us.

The Holy Spirit Draws Us to Jesus

The first thing the Holy Spirit does is draw us to Jesus so that we can be saved. Salvation is the starting point in the redemption process. Jesus is the firstborn Son of God and is the picture and example of what God intends us to be as sons. We begin with being saved and then walk out the transformation into the fully grown, spiritual person we are meant to be.

In our sinful nature, it is not our tendency to seek God. Many people avoid Him or pretend He doesn't exist, but the Holy Spirit works to soften hearts and draw people to God by showing God's goodness to them. The Word of God says that it is the goodness of God that leads people to repentance or a change of heart.

The apostles and believers down through the centuries preached and explained salvation through faith in Jesus Christ. Through the message told, the Holy Spirit is able to reveal God's mercy and goodness to people so that they may be saved.

Everyone must be saved and born again by the Spirit of God because we cannot be right with God by our efforts to keep the Law. We must believe in the saving blood of Jesus to save us and make us right with God. When someone is born again, the Holy Spirit enters that person's heart and makes a new creation: a child of God. The Spirit will never leave nor forsake that person.

Salvation brings us into relationship with God, which is the whole purpose of being redeemed. He becomes our Father and we His children. We are made His family, and other believers become our brothers and sisters. This is a family of love, joined together by His Holy Spirit—what God wanted and intended from the beginning.

> *This is the message of faith that we proclaim: If you confess with your mouth, "Jesus is Lord," and believe in your heart that God raised Him from the dead, you will be saved. One believes with the heart, resulting in righteousness, and one confesses with the mouth, resulting in salvation.*
> —Rom. 10:8–10 HCSB

The Holy Spirit Helps Get the Message Out

Since people are lost and their hearts are hard toward God, it is challenging to get them to listen to the truth about God's love. We can talk ourselves blue in the face trying to convince people, but God knew it would take a special power to get past the barriers. The Holy Spirit brings His presence and ability into the scene to get the job done. For someone to be saved, there must be a willing believer who will speak the message to the lost. Once there is a speaker, the Holy Spirit will help train and equip the messenger and fill his mouth with the right words to speak the good news. The supernatural ability of the Holy Spirit will co-labor with the believing disciple to give power to enlighten and save the hearer of the message.

Romans 10:14–15, 17 describes the process involved:

> *But how can they call on Him they have not believed? And how can they believe without hearing about Him? And how can they hear without a preacher? And how can they preach unless they are sent? . . . So faith comes from what is heard, and what is heard comes through the message about Christ* (HCSB).

Jesus commissioned His church to tell this message of salvation to every person because He does not want anyone to be lost. That is a daunting task—there is no way we are up to the challenge on our own. Jesus knew that and sent us help. Through the Holy Spirit, He gave His church the tools needed to do it.

The Holy Spirit Empowers

When Jesus departed to heaven, the very last thing He told the disciples to do was wait in Jerusalem to be equipped for living their new spiritual lives. This equipping would bring help to their personal lives and also enable them to help other people. It would fulfill one of the promises God had made to mankind long ago. It would be the pouring out of the Holy Spirit on believers so that they would be witnesses of what Jesus had done and so that they could live in power. The equipping would be an encounter with the Holy Spirit beyond what they had experienced in salvation and in being born again. It would mirror what Jesus experienced at His own baptism so that they could follow in His footsteps and live and minister as He did. This life-changing event happened during the Jewish festival known as Pentecost, just ten days after Jesus's ascension to heaven.

> *While He was together with them, He commanded them not to leave Jerusalem, but to wait for the Father's promise, "This," He said, "is what you heard from Me; for John baptized with water, but you will be baptized with the Holy Spirit not many days from now. . . . But you will receive power when the Holy Spirit has come on you, and you will be My witnesses in Jerusalem, in all Judea and Samaria, and to the ends of the earth."*
> —Acts 1:4–5, 8 HCSB

Noah Webster's 1828 edition of the *American Dictionary of the English Language* defines *Pentecost* as:

1. "A solemn festival of the Jews, so called because celebrated on the fiftieth day after the sixteenth of Nisan, which was the second day of the Passover. It was called the feast of weeks, because it was celebrated seven weeks after the Passover. It was instituted to oblige the people to repair to the temple of the Lord, there to acknowledge his absolute dominion over the country, and offer him the first fruits of their harvest; also that they might call to mind and give thanks to God for the law which he had given them at Sinai on the fiftieth day from their departure from Egypt."

2. "Whitsuntide, a solemn feast of the church, held in commemoration of the descent of the Holy Spirit on the apostles."

Interestingly, as noted in the first definition, the Law had been given to the Israelites fifty days after leaving Egypt, and Pentecost became associated with remembering the giving of the Law. Pentecost, a day of law, is the day God chose to pour out His Holy Spirit on mankind. This is not a coincidence—God orchestrates everything perfectly. In His mercy, a festival associated with the Law became a day of pouring out God's Spirit and ushering in grace.

Man had been under the Law for centuries without pleasing God. Now the Spirit was being poured out to give man a new freedom and power beyond anything Adam and Eve experienced. Jesus Christ was an end to the Law for salvation. As Romans 10:4 states, "For Christ is the end of the law for righteousness to everyone who believes." Jesus brought a new way for God to deal with people. You see, faith in the blood of Jesus brought grace, experienced by the Spirit, resulting in eternal life.

Galatians 3:21–22 explains that life came back to man not by the Law, but by the promised Holy Spirit:

> *Is the Law then contrary to the promises of God? May it never be! For if a law had been given which was able to impart life, then righteousness would indeed have been based on law. But the Scripture has shut up everyone under sin, so that the promise by faith in Jesus Christ might be given to those who believe.*

Acts 2:1–4 further describes what happened when the Holy Spirit was poured out in the earth:

> *When the day of Pentecost had arrived, they were all together in one place. Suddenly a sound like that of a violent rushing wind came from heaven, and it filled the whole house where they were staying. And tongues, like flames of fire that were divided, appeared to them and rested on each one of them. Then they were all filled with the Holy Spirit and began to speak in different languages, as the Spirit gave them ability for speech* (HCSB).

People from all parts of the world were in Jerusalem that day celebrating Pentecost. As the Holy Spirit descended on the disciples, they were able to speak in other languages they did not know, and all the visitors could understand what was being said in their own languages. By the supernatural power and ability of the Holy Spirit, the disciples told about the mighty works of God. As a result, thousands of people heard the message of redemption accomplished by Jesus Christ. They believed and were saved.

As explained in the second definition of Pentecost quoted from *Webster's*, Pentecost was also a feast of the "first fruits" of the harvest. Fittingly, the disciples experienced the first fruits of the harvest that day, with the fruit being a harvest of souls for the Kingdom of God. Three thousand people believed in Jesus Christ and were born again, and this was just the start of the mighty things the Spirit of God would achieve on the earth.

With the power of the Holy Spirit, the disciples preached and taught the people. God confirmed their message with signs and miracles, and multitudes were healed, saved, and filled with the Holy Spirit. As the message of redemption continued to spread, the church grew exponentially. Acts 5:12–16 tells us:

> *At the hands of the apostles many signs and wonders were taking place among the people; and they were all with one accord in Solomon's portico. But none of the rest dared to associate with them; however, the people held them in high esteem. And all the more believers in the Lord, multitudes of men and women, were constantly added* to their number; *to such an extent that they even carried the sick out into the streets and laid them on cots and pallets, so that when Peter came by at least his shadow might fall on any one of them. Also the people from the cities in the vicinity of Jerusalem were coming together, bringing people who were sick or af-flicted with unclean spirits, and they were all being healed.*

The Holy Spirit accomplished mighty acts then—signs and wonders, healings, and miracles, saving people and making them into sons of God. He still performs these mighty wonders today.

Baptism in the Holy Spirit

After we are saved and born again by the Holy Spirit, we are to follow the early believers' experience of being baptized in the Holy Spirit, which brings power and the ability to overcome into our lives. He is our help throughout our earthly life as we journey from the natural man to our completed spiritual man.

Being born again is an indwelling of the Spirit, and you cannot be born again apart from the Holy Spirit. According to Romans 8:9–10:

> *However, you are not in the flesh but in the Spirit, if indeed the Spirit of God dwells in you. But if anyone does not have the Spirit of Christ, he does not belong to Him. If Christ is in you, though the body is dead because of sin, yet the spirit is alive because of righteousness.*

Beyond the Spirit's work of salvation, baptism in the Holy Spirit is an anointing that comes upon a person and covers him with the power of God—a smearing on of God's supernatural ability. Following are just a few accounts of believers being baptized in the Holy Spirit.

> *Now when the apostles in Jerusalem heard that Samaria had received the word of God, they sent them Peter and John, who came down and prayed for them, that they might receive the Holy Spirit. For He had not yet fallen upon any of them; they had simply been baptized in the name of the Lord Jesus. Then they began laying their hands on them, and they were receiving the Holy Spirit.*

—Acts 8:14–17

While Peter was still speaking these words, the Holy Spirit fell upon all those who were listening to the message [of salvation]. All the circumcised believers who had come with Peter were amazed, because the gift of the Holy Spirit had been poured out upon the Gentiles also. For they were hearing them speaking with tongues and exalting God. Then Peter answered, "Surely no one can refuse the water for these to be baptized who have received the Holy Spirit just as we did, can he?" And he ordered them to be baptized in the name of Jesus Christ. Then they asked him to stay on for a few days.

—Acts 10:44–48

It happened that while Apollos was at Corinth, Paul passed through the upper country and came to Ephesus, and found some disciples. He said to them, "Did you receive the Holy Spirit when you believed?" And they said to him, "No, we have not even heard whether there is a Holy Spirit." And he said, "Into what then were you baptized?" And they said, "Into John's baptism." Paul said, "John baptized with the baptism of repentance, telling the people to believe in Him who was coming after him, that is, in Jesus." When they heard this, they were baptized in the name of the Lord Jesus. And when Paul had laid his hands upon them, the Holy Spirit came on them, and they began speaking with tongues and prophesying.

—Acts 19:1–6

Whenever the Holy Spirit comes upon people, He always brings special supernatural gifts that help individuals in their daily walk. Every time the Holy Spirit came upon people throughout the book of Acts, the first gift He gave was the gift of speaking in tongues. At other times, as in Acts 19:6, the gift of prophesying was also given. Sometimes, the tongues were manifested as specific earthly languages, as on the day of Pentecost. Other times, the tongues were manifested as an unknown heavenly language that the Spirit spoke through believers to pray for them. The same is true today, a topic we will discuss later in the book.

Doing What Is Right: A New Way of Life

Another help the Holy Spirit gives is to help us to distinguish what is right and what is wrong so that we can have strength to overcome and do what is right.

There are two basic laws that rule the universe. These laws are covered in Romans 8:2: "For the law of the Spirit of life in Christ Jesus has set you free from the law of sin and of death." All other laws flow under them and from them, and these laws are unalterable.

- *The Law of Sin and Death:* When one sins, death is the consequence. The Ten Commandments, the Jewish laws, and governmental laws all give power to the Law of Sin and Death. Punishment or death is always the end result for breaking this law.
- *The Law of the Spirit of Life:* The Law of the Spirit of Life always brings life. Obedience to this Law results in blessings: joy, love, peace, prosperity, and goodness. The laws of forgiveness, love, and grace are under the Law of the Spirit of Life.

Man started out under the Law of the Spirit of Life, but when he sinned, he came under the jurisdiction of the Law of Sin and Death.

Escape from the Law of Sin and Death can only come through Jesus Christ. He fulfilled the requirement of this law by dying for sin—not His sin, but our sin. Being made a man, He is a champion for man. As the representative for all mankind, the punishment He endured for sin was credited to men and women who receive His substitutionary death for them. We are brought out from under the Law of Sin and Death and brought under the jurisdiction of the Law of the Spirit of Life only by being joined to Jesus and receiving His Spirit. His Spirit brings life into us when we believe in His shed blood to save us.

The question will arise: Since we are right with God through faith in the blood of Jesus and are forgiven and under the Law of the Spirit of life, why be concerned about sinning or keeping the rules?

Are you having a memory lapse? Sinning is what got us into a mess to begin with! Even though we are unable to keep the rules in our own strength, God has made a way for us to live holy. It is by our Helper, the Holy Spirit. The law is good and perfect, and in our glorified bodies, we will be transformed into the exact image of Jesus, who never sinned and who kept the law totally. We will be like Him—righteous people made perfect (Hebrews 12:23). But for now, we have been joined with Jesus through His Spirit, and because of that union, we have died with Him to sin.

Romans 8:3 says that God actually condemned (judged and put to death) sin in the flesh in the body of Jesus. Sin has already been paid for in the body of Christ and has no right to control us since we have joined in Jesus's death through His Spirit.

> *Or do you not know that all of us who have been baptized into Christ Jesus have been baptized into His death? Therefore we have been buried with Him through baptism into death, so that as Christ was raised from the dead through the glory of the Father, so we too might walk in newness of life. . . . Knowing this, that our old self was crucified with Him, in order that our body of sin might be done away with, that we should no longer be slaves to sin.*
>
> —Rom. 6:3–4, 6

Through our powerful union with the Holy Spirit, we are told to put to death the sinful deeds of our body. As we submit to and follow the leading of the Holy Spirit, He enables us to live right when we struggle against the desires of our flesh. We are under God's loving grace and forgiveness, but doing good is still good and is what every good Father wants for His children. We have the power of the Holy Spirit—let's draw on Him to do what is right!

Romans 8 is another wonderful passage in the Bible. It tells much of how the Holy Spirit helps us in our journey toward eternity: "Therefore, no condemnation now exists for those in Christ Jesus, because the Spirit's law of life in Christ Jesus has set you free from the law of sin and of death" (Romans 8:1–2 HCSB).

Yes, the Spirit is life. We are no longer under the dominion of sin with the penalty of death.

Right Thinking Leads to Right Acting

If we think right, our actions will follow. God's word is truth and always teaches us what is right. When we allow the Spirit to direct our thought life, our emotions and actions will come in alignment with what God says is right. For example, Romans 8:5–7 tells us to set our minds on spiritual things and not on things of the flesh, while Galatians 5 clearly draws the line between fleshly thoughts and spiritual thoughts.

Regarding fleshly thoughts, don't spend your time thinking about these things:

> *Now the deeds of the flesh are evident, which are: immorality, impurity, sensuality, idolatry, sorcery, enmities, strife, jealousy, outbursts of anger, disputes, dissensions, factions, envying, drunkenness, carousing, and things like these, of which I forewarn you, just as I have forewarned you, that those who practice such things shall not inherit the kingdom of God.*
> —Gal. 5:19–21

Instead, spend your time focusing on these spiritual thoughts:

> *But the fruit of the Spirit is love, joy, peace, patience, kindness, goodness, faithfulness, gentleness, self-control; against such things there is no law. Now those who belong to Christ Jesus have crucified the flesh with its passions and desires. If we live by the Spirit, let us also walk by the Spirit.*
> —Gal. 5:22–25

By listening to the Holy Spirit and drawing on His power to obey, we are putting the flesh and its deeds to death and replacing the bad with the good. How do we listen to the Holy Spirit? By being still so that He can whisper to our spirits or give us a knowing in our hearts.

We not only are declared right by the Spirit through Jesus's blood, but we also learn to live right by the Spirit. Thinking the Spirit's way will change us into the image of Jesus. Stop doing the wrong that you lust to do—the Spirit in you wants to do what is right.

Right thinking frees us from many fears and things that hold us in bondage. Listening to the Holy Spirit's leading and obeying His direction will always bring peace to our hearts. Romans 8:15–17 says:

> *For you have not received a spirit of slavery leading to fear again, but you have received a spirit of adoption as sons by which we cry out, "Abba! Father!" The Spirit Himself testifies with our spirit that we are children of God, and if children, heirs also, heirs of God and fellow heirs with Christ, if indeed we suffer with Him so that we may also be glorified with Him.*

Perseverance

The Holy Spirit helps us persevere through the difficulties of the physical life as the flesh and spirit struggle against each other. We do have an enemy, and being saved does not eliminate trouble from our lives. But the Holy Spirit strengthens and reassures us, teaching us how to stand firm against the devil and overcome him. We have victory through the blood of Jesus Christ as we testify in agreement with the Word of God. Perseverance and faith have great reward. As we stand firm, God turns things around and works everything together for our good (Romans 8:28). And, as our ultimate hope, the Holy Spirit assures us of future glory when the sons of God will be revealed to all creation—when our earthly body will be traded in for an eternal spiritual body.

Romans 8:19, 23–25 further explains this idea:

> *For the anxious longing of the creation waits eagerly for the revealing of the sons of God. . . . And not only this, but also we ourselves, having the first fruits of the Spirit, even we ourselves groan within ourselves, waiting eagerly for our adoption as sons, the redemption of our body. For in hope we have been saved, but hope that is seen is not hope; for who hopes for what he already sees? But if we hope for what we do not see, with perseverance we wait eagerly for it.*

Praying for Us

Another help of the Holy Spirit is His prayers for us. With our own thinking and emotions, we do a very poor job of praying God's will. Many times, we are just rehearsing our problems and worries, and we really don't even know where to begin. Moreover, much of what we pray is not in faith that God is taking care of our requests because often our problems seem so much bigger than God. God knows we are weak in our ability to produce results. The Holy Spirit intercedes for us to accomplish God's best for us. God has much to say about prayer, but in this book, we will focus only on the Spirit's role. Romans 8:26–28 tells us:

> *In the same way the Spirit also helps our weakness; for we do not know how to pray as we should, but the Spirit Himself intercedes for us with groanings too deep for words;*

and He who searches the hearts knows what the mind of the Spirit is, because He intercedes for the saints according to the will of God. And we know that God causes all things to work together for good to those who love God, to those who are called according to His purpose.

At the time of our baptism in the Holy Spirit, God lauds us with an immeasurably valuable gift when He gives us the treasure of speaking in tongues. The category of tongues talked about in Romans 8:26–28 is a heavenly, spiritual language God gives us, made up of syllables and sounds the Spirit gives. This is the Holy Spirit's means of praying for us. When we yield our mouth to the Holy Spirit in prayer, He is able to speak His words through us from our innermost being, pouring forth what is really going on in our spirit, praying our real needs and desires. He bypasses our minds and emotions and gets to the heart of the matter. He knows God's will for us and what is best for us. The Holy Spirit prays our requests and needs out into the presence of the Father, and the Father works everything out for our good. We don't have to know all the details of what is being prayed, and it is best that we don't. We can simply rest in the truth that God is taking care of us, trusting the Spirit to bring us help and peace. At the same time, our enemy, the devil, doesn't understand what the Spirit is saying, so praying in tongues (praying in the Spirit) really helps to keep the devil's nose out of our business.

Thank you, Daddy, for such a wonderful gift and such a wonderful means of communicating with you!

The Holy Spirit Conforms Us to the Image of Jesus Christ

Jesus is the firstborn of God's sons. But guess what? God wants a bunch of sons like Him, and that is us. He means for us to resemble Jesus in every way. As we cooperate with the Holy Spirit, He changes us from glory to glory so that when we stand before the Father, we will be just like Jesus, made perfect through the blood of Jesus and the

Holy Spirit. As Romans 8:29 relates, "For those whom He foreknew, He also predestined *to become* conformed to the image of His Son, that He might be the firstborn among many brethren."

Personal Daily Help: The Comforter and Teacher

We discussed earlier how the Holy Spirit gives us personal help. He wants to help us in every area of our lives, from start to finish—the same help that the early believers had is available for us. Simply ask the Holy Spirit to help you each day and believe He has heard and answered your request. He is our true and faithful helper and companion. He never fails us.

Another name for the Holy Spirit is the Comforter because He comes alongside us and fortifies us with His presence. As we commune with Him, His presence brings peace, strength, revelation of truth, joy, and real comfort in the midst of everyday life and challenges. He is our teacher and brings to our remembrance what Jesus has said. He also reveals the mysteries of God as we read and feed on His Word. The Holy Spirit has revealed these secret mysteries of God and His redemption plan that were hidden throughout the ages so that they can be spread throughout the world.

The Bible tells us we have the mind of Christ so that we can know His thoughts and heart's desires and act in line with what He wants. This knowledge is given through the Holy Spirit. The Holy Spirit is called the Spirit of Truth, and He leads and guides us into all truth.

Good Gifts

Through the Holy Spirit, God gives His children good gifts. Like any good Father, God gives gifts that benefit and delight His children, gifts that are spiritual and have immense value for living life to the fullest. Many times, children do not appreciate the gifts they receive, nor do they fully know how to use them. But the Holy Spirit is the Teacher and will also help us implement His gifts in our lives. These gifts include the word of wisdom, the word of knowledge, faith, gifts of healing, miracles, prophecy, distinguishing of spirits, tongues, and interpretation of tongues (1 Corinthians 12:4–11). All these gifts are wonderful in helping us develop into the full image of Christ.

Additionally, God gifts us with special people in our lives who help us to grow up into the fine sons He desires. The Holy Spirit then works through these people to train us. We are helped immensely to mature in Christ by those who are apostles, prophets, teachers, evangelists, workers of miracles, workers of healings, those with gifts of helps, and those with gifts of administrations (1 Corinthians 12:28).

Knowing God

God honors us by giving us His indwelling Spirit. The Bible tells us that it is only the spirit of a man who lives in him that really knows that man and his concerns. Likewise, it is only the Spirit of God who knows the concerns and heart of God. In turn, we have the same Spirit, and by having God's Spirit come live in us, we can intimately know God, His heart and concerns, and what He has given to us.

> *But as it is written: What eye did not see and ear did not hear, and what never entered the human mind—God prepared this for those who love Him. Now God has revealed these things to us by the Spirit, for the Spirit searches everything, even the depths of God. For who among men knows the thoughts of a man except the spirit of the man that is in him? In the same way, no one knows the thoughts of God except the Spirit of God. Now we have not received the spirit of the world, but the Spirit who comes from God, so that we may understand what has been freely given to us by God.*
> —1 Cor. 2:9–12 HCSB

What an awesome relationship the Father has birthed us into. As the best of Fathers, He has put His own Holy Spirit into us to care for us: to train, guide, bless, and comfort us; to fellowship with us; and to give us good gifts. The Father teaches His children to be like Him, and His children have the privilege of spending eternity with Him.

The Father is God. Jesus is God's Word to us. He is everything God has to say to us. The Holy Spirit is God's life. He lives in us. The three are all one God. They cannot be separated. And by God's Spirit, we have been joined together to be made one with them— sons of God forever.

Chapter 17

Revealing of the Sons of God—Redemption Complete

E arlier, I described how the Jewish people celebrated the Day of Atonement, with the high priest entering the Holy of Holies in the tent of meeting. The high priest met with God through the blood of animals so that man's sins would be covered, so that there would be communion with God and to hear what He had to say. Believers today have become the meeting place with God, His Holy Spirit living and communing in them because of the blood of Jesus. So today we can each say:

> I have become the tent of meeting—the Holy of Holies where God meets above the mercy seat because of the blood of Jesus. I have washed my body and put on clean clothes (represented in baptism). I approach His presence with the sweet incense of faith and worship. I come before the mercy seat of God with the blood of Jesus the Lamb with faith that it covers and pays for and wipes out my sin. The Spirit of God descends into my heart to live in my tent (being) forever. Jesus has

become my scapegoat, my propitiation, and carried my sin away into a deserted place, never to be seen again. I will never appear in court to be judged and condemned or to meet His wrath, for I have met at His mercy seat of love and been made new—a son of God.

We started this book by saying that God wanted sons who were redeemable and who would choose to love and obey Him and never fall to be eternally condemned and cast from His presence. God has done the work. Redemption is nearly complete. God will soon restore all things. Eternity is at hand. So, let's look at the unveiling of His sons.

Man was created a physical being with a spirit and a soul made to live in a body. With the possibility that man would sin, the body was made in a way that could become subject to death, so that a redeemed soul could shed its natural body and take up residence in a new spiritual body. In God's wisdom, when man sinned, he was made to die. The old body just won't do for eternity. Corruptible has to put on incorruption. When the sons of God are revealed, redeemed persons will have their natural bodies exchanged for a marvelous new, eternal, spiritual body that is free from degeneration, aging, sickness, pain, and disease—one that will never die.

Our future is so bright. All the problems of this life dim next to what glory is going to be revealed to us as we are changed from the natural to the spiritual being. We quote again from Romans 8:18–21:

> For I consider that the sufferings of this present time are not worthy to be compared with the glory that is to be revealed to us. For the anxious longing of the creation waits eagerly for the revealing of the sons of God. For the creation was subjected to futility, not willingly, but because of Him who subjected it, in hope that the creation itself also will be set free from its slavery to corruption into the freedom of the glory of the children of God.

A lot of questions can enter our minds. What are the sons of God going to be like? What about the people who have died? What about people who are still alive? What does the Word say?

We must remember that Jesus came to show us the way. If we keep our eyes on Him, we can walk confidently. Jesus has already trod the path. Christ has been raised from the dead, and we will be like Him.

> *But now Christ has been raised from the dead, the first fruits of those who are asleep. For since by a man came death, by a man also came the resurrection of the dead. For as in Adam all die, so also in Christ all will be made alive. But each in his own order: Christ the first fruits, after that those who are Christ's at His coming, then comes the end, when He hands over the kingdom to the God and Father, when He has abolished all rule and all authority and power. For He must reign until He has put all His enemies under His feet. The last enemy that will be abolished is death.*
>
> —1 Cor. 15:20–26

God tells us that our glorified bodies are going to be totally different from what we have now. We can only imagine. We do know it will be like Jesus's body, for we are being made into His image and we will see Him as He is.

> *But someone will say, "How are the dead raised? What kind of body will they have when they come?" Foolish one! What you sow does not come to life unless it dies. And as for what you sow—you are not sowing the future body, but only a seed, perhaps of wheat or another grain. But God gives it a body as He wants, and to each of the seeds its own body. Not all flesh is the same flesh; there*

is one flesh for humans, another for animals, another for birds, and another for fish. There are heavenly bodies and earthly bodies, but the splendor of the heavenly bodies is different from that of the earthly ones. There is a splendor of the sun, another of the moon, and another of the stars; for one star differs from another star in splendor. So it is with the resurrection of the dead: Sown in corruption, raised in incorruption; sown in dishonor, raised in glory; sown in weakness, raised in power; sown a natural body, raised a spiritual body. If there is a natural body, there is also a spiritual body. So it is written: The first man Adam became a living being; the last Adam became a life-giving Spirit. However, the spiritual is not first, but the natural; then the spiritual. The first man was from the earth and made of dust; the second man is from heaven. Like the man made of dust, so are those who are made of dust; like the heavenly man, so are those who are heavenly. And just as we have borne the image of the man made of dust, we will also bear the image of the heavenly man.

—1 Cor. 15:35–49 HCSB

So how does this all take place? Jesus told us that as we near the end of time as we know it, we are to be on the outlook for His return to earth. There will be signs for us to observe. The main one is the restoration of the nation of Israel. This has already taken place, so the time is drawing ever closer. It is a whole separate study that we will not explore in this book. However, do your studying and watch for His return. Jesus will return very suddenly, and specific things will happen. The most exciting thing is the revelation of the sons of God.

First Corinthians 15 tells us that we will be instantly changed from a natural body to a spiritual body. Some believers will have already died, but some will still be alive on the earth.

Behold, I tell you a mystery; we will not all sleep, but we will all be changed, in a moment, in the twinkling of an eye, at the last trumpet; for the trumpet will sound, and the dead will be raised imperishable, and we will be changed. For this perishable must put on the imperishable, and this mortal must put on immortality. But when this perishable will have put on the imperishable, and this mortal will have put on immortality, then will come about the saying that is written, "DEATH IS SWALLOWED UP IN VICTORY. O DEATH, WHERE IS YOUR VICTORY? O DEATH, WHERE IS YOUR STING?" The sting of death is sin, and the power of sin is the law; but thanks be to God, who gives us the victory through our Lord Jesus Christ.

—1 Cor. 15:51–57

Upon Jesus's return, believers will be caught up into heaven to meet Him and be changed into a spiritual body. This is frequently known as the Rapture or catching away. These sons of God will attend the marriage supper of the Lamb, where they will be joined to Jesus forever. It will be a celebration that lasts seven years.

Those who have not been born again through believing in the blood of Jesus will be left on the earth to undergo a great time of trouble. It will be very costly to become a believer during this trying time. Most people who decide to follow Jesus will be martyred. Those left behind on the earth will see the devil taking a strong stand against mankind, bringing persecution, death, and destruction. It will also be a time when God pours out His righteous wrath on those who have refused to believe in His Son.

At the end of seven years, Jesus Christ will come back with His bride (the sons of God) to put a stop to all rebellion on the earth. He will set up His righteous rule on the earth for a thousand years, with the sons of God partaking in the administration of His government. The devil will be bound from acting during the thousand years and will not be allowed to interfere with man.

At the end of the thousand years, the devil will be released from captivity and allowed to briefly test earth's inhabitants. These will be those who have populated the earth during the one thousand years while the devil has been restrained and who have not previously been given the opportunity to choose between obeying God or rejecting Him. Most will choose rebellion. In Revelation 20:7–9, we see the rebellion that takes place:

> *When the thousand years are completed, Satan will be released from his prison, and will come out to deceive the nations which are in the four corners of the earth, Gog and Magog, to gather them together for the war; the number of them is like the sand of the seashore. And they came up on the broad plain of the earth and surrounded the camp of the saints and the beloved city, and fire came down from heaven and devoured them.*

God puts an end to it all. The devil will be permanently judged and cast into the lake of fire, along with those people who have refused to believe God.

We as believers, the sons of God, will experience wonderful things. We will:

- Have our bodies changed into spiritual bodies that will never die (1 Corinthians 15:51–57; Philippians 3:20–21).
- Be married to Christ (Revelation 19:7–9).
- Rule and reign with Jesus (Romans 5:17; Ephesians 2:4–7; Mark 10:40; Revelation 20:4).
- See the devil destroyed (Revelation 20:10).
- Be rewarded for what we have done on earth in our natural bodies and lives. (1 Corinthians 3:8; Revelation 22:12).
- Escape the Great White Throne judgment where nonbelievers are righteously judged by the Law. They will receive the wrath of God for not believing in the blood of Jesus that provided

grace and forgiveness for them. Their final place will be in the lake of fire with the devil, experiencing horrendous torture. This is the second death. They are doubly dead because they never were born again—never having been brought to life by the Holy Spirit. They are eternally condemned to death and terrible torment in the lake of fire (Revelation 20:11–15).

- Escape the second death (Revelation 20:5–7).
- Judge angels (1 Corinthians 6:2–3).
- Live in the New Jerusalem forever with God, and He will be our light. It is a city beyond description (Revelation 21:10–27).
- Be like our Father and His Son, Jesus, forever, with no chance of ever falling again. (Revelation 22:3–5).

Let's take a few minutes to look at the glory of God we will experience in the future as sons of God in the heavenly realm. So often we see heaven portrayed as a place where we float around on a cloud, playing a harp. That seems pretty boring and is a much different picture than what the Bible says. In Acts 2:21, we are told that heaven must be Jesus's abode until He restores all things. All that has been destroyed by the devil and sin will be made new, perfect, and eternal. Not only does that apply to our bodies, but to our future dwelling place and all it contains.

The new creation is described in Revelation 21 and 22. The new heaven and earth are brought forth, and the first heaven and earth pass away. The sea is gone, and a marvelous new and holy city is brought down from heaven for the habitation of God and His sons. Yes, God will dwell with men, and we will be His people, and He will be our God. There will be no more tears, death, grief, crying, or pain. All that will be over and done. Everything God is doing is a gift for His children.

The Holy City will be known as the New Jerusalem. It will be dressed in God's glory and shining like a very precious gem. It will have massive, high walls with twelve gates, each made of a single pearl. Angels will attend the gates, and the names of the twelve tribes of Israel will be written on those gates. The city wall will have twelve foundations, each made of a different precious gemstone. The construction material of the city itself will be something we have never beheld—pure gold like clear glass. The city will be huge, laid out in a square with its length, width, and height each measuring 1,400 miles. There will be room for everyone who has come to the Savior. The broad street of the city will be made of pure gold, like transparent glass.

God the Father and the Lord Jesus will be our sanctuary and dwelling place in that city. There will be no need for sun or moon there. Night will no longer exist, for the glory of God will light up the place. Nothing vile, evil, or imperfect will ever enter the city— only those whose names have been written with the blood of the Lamb in the Lamb's Book of Life.

We will drink living water, flowing like a river from the throne of God and from Jesus, the Lamb's throne, down the middle of the city's street. We will eat from the tree of life growing on both sides of the river. We will joyfully serve our God and look upon His loving face. We will be His and reign and rule with Him forever. Praise God!

Chapter 18

Who Is God to Me, and What Is My Response?

We have talked about how you can be saved and born again. But how do you get to know God as your Father? Time spent together is what builds a relationship. As we interact, we get to know each other, become familiar with each other's ways, likes, and dislikes, and we learn to trust each other. As you spend time with God each day reading what He has to say in His Word and talking with Him in prayer, you will get to know our Father more intimately.

Our relationship with God is built on faith. Faith is what pleases our Father. He wants us to believe what He says and put our full trust in Him. He no longer responds to us in wrath as the angry judge. We now know Him as a good, loving Father. The more you think of Him as being good to you personally all the time, the more you will experience His goodness. He delights in responding to your positive expectation.

When bad experiences do come your way, you must resist the temptation to think they are given you by God. There are other explanations for the sources of bad things. We must remember that we live in a fallen world where sin is rampant. Because of that, accidents happen, people get sick, and bad weather causes damage. God did not cause these things—the rebellion of mankind brought these maladies into the world.

People have freedom to make their own choices, and many times the choices they make bring bad consequences. God does not control our choices. If you choose to drink and drive and have an accident, God is not going to jump in front of your car to stop you.

We must also remember that we have an adversary, the devil, who brings much trouble into our paths. His purpose is to make us doubt God and keep us from salvation. Persevere. Never, ever, ever give up. God is faithful to you. He will see you through.

The wonderful thing we must remember is that we have a Helper, the Holy Spirit, in the midst of all life's circumstances. We must not blame God for troubles. Instead, we must act like we really believe God is our Helper. We simply must ask Him for help and believe He has heard us. He is for us and will work things together for our good. He will show us how to stand in all situations and how to take appropriate steps in doing His will and in resisting the evil that comes our way.

The Holy Spirit will help us to rest and have peace in the time of trouble. Hebrews 4 tells us that there is a believer's rest for us. We can cast our cares on Him because He cares for us. We can experience the reality that God never leaves us nor forsakes us and that He is faithful in all His ways to us. He has a light load and an easy yoke for us.

Read the Bible every day. It is God's instruction manual and love letter to us. His Spirit will give you understanding of what you read. Agree with what God says in His Word. It is truth, even when your own thinking may not be the same as He says. Reading and speaking God's Word will build faith in you. As you speak out His Word in faith, He will do it. God tells us in the Bible, "I am watching over My word to perform it" (Jeremiah 1:12).

Read a chapter, section, or book of the Bible over and over until it comes to life in you. Find out what the words mean; use a good dictionary. Ponder and meditate on the verses; look at it from all directions and in connection with other verses around it. God will reveal wonderful things to you, and it will change your life.

Spend time praying—talking and listening to God throughout the day. He will whisper into your heart His love and truth and show you the way to go. Take time to thank and praise Him for His goodness. The Bible tells us that God inhabits the praises of His people.

Spend time each day praying in tongues, allowing God's Spirit to pray through you. He will pray out God's plan for you and those you pray for, bringing the spiritual into manifestation in the natural. You are allowing the Spirit to pray out and orchestrate the future through you. As the Spirit prays, He will bring you revelation and provide a way.

Step out in obedience to what God tells you to do. He will meet you there and back you up with His provision and power. It is His response to faith. You are very valuable to God. The proof is that He spent His own blood to buy you back from your evil way of life. How can you put a price on God's blood! So, don't worry—take it to God in prayer with thanksgiving. Doesn't He feed the birds, and they certainly don't worry. You are worth more than many birds.

You are a part of the Body of Christ—the Church. You may be a hand or a foot or an ear. Each part needs the other, and all parts need Jesus, the head. No part is independent of the others. So, it is important that you ask the Holy Spirit to lead you to a local church that accurately teaches the Word of God and operates in the Holy Spirit and love. The Holy Spirit is the life of the body and operates through the body.

God will fit you into the Church in the right place. You will learn truths for life and godliness there and come to know God better than you can on your own. God will give you many opportunities to love and obey and give. With the gift of other believers that God gives us for our help, you can grow into the image of Christ that God intends you to be. He gives us those who are apostles, pastors, teachers, evangelists, and prophets who can give us instruction and be godly examples. There is something very special about God's family coming together to pray and worship Him and love one another. God says that where two or three are gathered in His name that He is in the midst of them.

So speak right, love others, love God, tell others the redemption story, sing, laugh, be happy, trust, obey God, give it your all, don't give up, pray always, work, rest, spend much time with God, rejoice, meditate on the Word, admit your mistakes, say what God says, do what is right, listen to God's Spirit, ask and expect to receive. Fulfill the whole plan God has for your life.

You are a Son of God!

It is my sincere prayer that you see God as He really is and see yourself as He sees you till we all come to the full stature of Christ, experiencing the glory of God together.

REDEEMED!

_____

Now unto him that is able to keep you from falling,
and to present you faultless before the presence of his glory
with exceeding joy, to the only wise God our Saviour,
be glory and majesty, dominion and power,
both now and ever. Amen.
—Jude 24–25 (KJV)

_____

Conclusion

When we began this book, we talked about the importance of God's righteousness. He remains true to His righteous character. He has provided the way to deal with you righteously in grace as a loving father. If you reject His Son, He will righteously deal with you in wrath as a just judge enforcing His Law. God's righteousness has clearly been revealed and upheld: Righteous wrath to those who do not believe. Righteous grace to those who receive Jesus as the one who purchased them with His blood.

The great day of the Lord is soon coming when the sons of God will be revealed, and the sons of the devil will be exposed.

Now is the time to make your choice. Which one are you? This is your time to respond to God's invitation.

If you believe in your heart that God raised Jesus from the dead and confess with your mouth that Jesus is Lord, you will be saved. We invite you now to call on the Lord Jesus Christ with the prayer below and be redeemed:

> Jesus, I believe that You are the Son of God. I have faith in Your precious blood that You shed to pay for my sins. I believe that You rose from the dead declaring me cleared of my sin. I receive You as my Savior and Lord. Come into my heart by Your Holy Spirit and make me born again, a son of God.
>
> Holy Spirit, I ask that You baptize me with Your presence. Come upon me with the evidence of speaking in tongues, anointing me to walk in Your power. Thank You, Father, for Your wonderful redemption. Amen.

www.ingramcontent.com/pod-product-compliance
Lightning Source LLC
Chambersburg PA
CBHW071754090426
42737CB00012B/1820